A DAY IN
TOKYO

A DAY IN
TOKYO

A Japanese cookbook

Brendan Liew & Caryn Ng

Smith
Street
Books

EARLY

14

MID

52

LATE

146

BASICS

214

INTRODUCTION

The Narita Express weaves its way from the airport towards Tokyo, the landscape slowly changing from countryside greenery to modernist apartments, illuminated billboards and the neon lights synonymous with the city. Tokyo Sky Tree comes into view, a sign that the train is reaching its destination.

It is impossible to not get distracted arriving in Tokyo Station. Vibrantly coloured eki-ben (train station bentō) glimmer in refrigerated cases – pops of yellow and orange from kinshi-tamago (omelette), ikura (salmon roe) and uni (sea urchin). Models of Japanese sweets, from mochi to regional specialties, beckon – a hint at what can be found within the mounds of exquisitely wrapped boxes the Japanese buy as gifts.

There are molten cheesecakes, baumkuchen, matcha langue du chat, sand cookies, roll cakes and a variety of Tokyo Bananas – mini banana-shaped sponge cakes filled with banana custard and stamped with a giraffe print (the original). There's a mesmerising taiyaki machine, in which fish-shaped iron moulds are filled with batter, red bean and custard, then grilled until golden. There's a ramen street and a Calbee shop selling fries – perfectly packed upright in a paper cup – and salty potato chips (crisps) drizzled with chocolate.

And that is just Tokyo station. You have yet to set foot outside.

It would be impossible to dine at every restaurant in Tokyo in a single lifetime. Layer upon layer of dining establishments exist here, stacked on top of each other in high-rise buildings, hidden down long, narrow alleyways and crammed tightly together in warrens. Their only signposts are noren, small-calligraphed signs accompanied by delicately arranged sprigs of flowers, or traditional Japanese lanterns hung outside the door.

Tokyo is a city where century-old restaurants can be found in-between modern ones; where third, fourth and fifth generations of chefs in neatly pressed white jackets live the life of shokunin (a word commonly translated as 'artisan' but which encapsulates so much more), going through the processes their forefathers went through before them.

It is here where a tofu restaurant sits within an Edo-era (1603–1868) compound with a koi pond and Japanese garden at the foot of Tokyo Tower. It is here where chefs at sleek, Japanese–French restaurants work against a backdrop of magnificent ikebana. And it is here where women in beautiful silk kimonos can be found gliding across private rooms in glass towers, carrying trays of antique tableware filled with exquisitely presented kaiseki dishes.

This is what makes Tokyo so enigmatic – its intoxicating blend of past and present, its balance of tradition and modernity.

It is in this city where Japan's chefs, trained in French, Italian and Spanish cuisines, return to blur the lines between Western and Japanese ingredients and techniques, and where Michelin-starred sushi chefs do a 180 and open up burger shops with traditionally grilled or battered fish sourced from Toyosu fish market. It is here where the modern incarnation of wagashi shops can be found selling traditional Japanese sweets, housed within striking architectural spaces by Tadao Ando and Kengo Kuma.

To perch at one of the city's hinoki (cypress wood) counters and have a beautifully assembled kakigori (shaved ice) or parfait, or stand in the tiny, sleek wooden space of Koffee Mameya enjoying a hand-dripped coffee, is an experience difficult to replicate anywhere else in the world.

But for every modern encounter Tokyo has to offer, we encourage you to take a step off the beaten path; to wander down laneways and slip behind norens; to soak in the serenity at Shinjuku Gyoen, Meiji Jingu or the city's countless other parks and tiny shrines; to explore shotengai (old shopping strips),

walk the streets of Yanaka and step through the old wooden doors of kissaten – beautiful dark-wood coffee shops of another era, often run by older generations; to eat menchi katsu (mince croquettes) from butcher shops and try wagashi from ancient wagashi-ya (wagashi purveyors).

Recently, we sat in a kissaten – Aroma Coffee Yaesu – in the quiet, almost forgotten Yaesuchika, an underground shopping mall inside Tokyo Station. Overhead, crowds rushed into each other for the local train lines and the Shinkansen: a world away from the serene, wood-wrapped space with its hand-dripped coffee, pizza toast and coffee jelly.

This is what makes us love Tokyo – the juxtaposition and harmonious existence of old and new. The trends of the West may have infiltrated the city, but Tokyo firmly puts its stamp on them.

In this book, we explore the food that makes this city: the traditional dishes that originated in Edo, as Japan's capital was known, to yōshoku (Japan's take on Western cuisine, stemming back to the Meiji era) and kaiseki (Japanese haute cuisine), traversing the city from hotcake breakfasts to late-night yakitori.

A NOTE FOR TRAVELLERS

In Tokyo, most foreign-friendly dining establishments have picture or English menus, or plastic food displays, which make it easy to simply point to what you'd like to eat. If at a loss, the word 'osusume', meaning 'recommend', is handy. Should you be greeted at the door by arms or fingers held up to form an 'X', make a polite retreat – it is the Japanese way of indicating that a restaurant is fully booked or does not accept foreigners or diners who do not have prior relationships with the restaurant.

Famous ramen restaurants often draw long lines: it's recommended to arrive 40 minutes or more before opening. As Japanese restaurants of all varieties are often small, seats are coveted, with some of the best places booking out months in advance. Hotel concierges are an excellent starting point for recommendations and restaurant bookings.

Finally, eating on the streets is considered impolite in Japan. One place you can find seating is the rooftops of department stores; Isetan in Shinjuku has a beautiful rooftop area with a small shrine and garden, where you can savour the delights from the depachika (department store food halls) below.

CHEF'S NOTES

Japanese cuisine is very flexible, and any protein can be substituted for another if you wish. For example, beef can replace pork in tonkatsu (it simply becomes gyūkatsu), and salt-grilled salmon can become salt-grilled whiting or mackerel. Meat in recipes can be substituted with tofu, mushrooms or other hearty vegetables such as daikon (Japanese radish) or pumpkin (winter squash).

We've used high-quality Japanese short-grain rice in this book (our favourite is Akita Komachi), but you can also use Californian-grown short-grain varieties. We have found these to give the best results, as the mild, delicately sweet flavour does not overpower the other ingredients. The water-to-rice ratio given in these recipes applies to this kind of rice. If you are using a different variety, the ratio may change.

- **Tablespoons are 15 ml (½ fl oz).**
- **Eggs are medium (60 g/2 oz).**
- **The oil is a neutral-flavoured oil such as rice bran, vegetable or canola.**
- **The salt is sea salt.**
- **Pepper is freshly ground.**
- **The olive oil is extra virgin olive oil.**
- **The soy sauce is Japanese dark soy sauce, or koikuchi shōyu, unless otherwise specified.**
- **Mayonnaise is Japanese mayonnaise (Kewpie preferably) unless otherwise specified.**

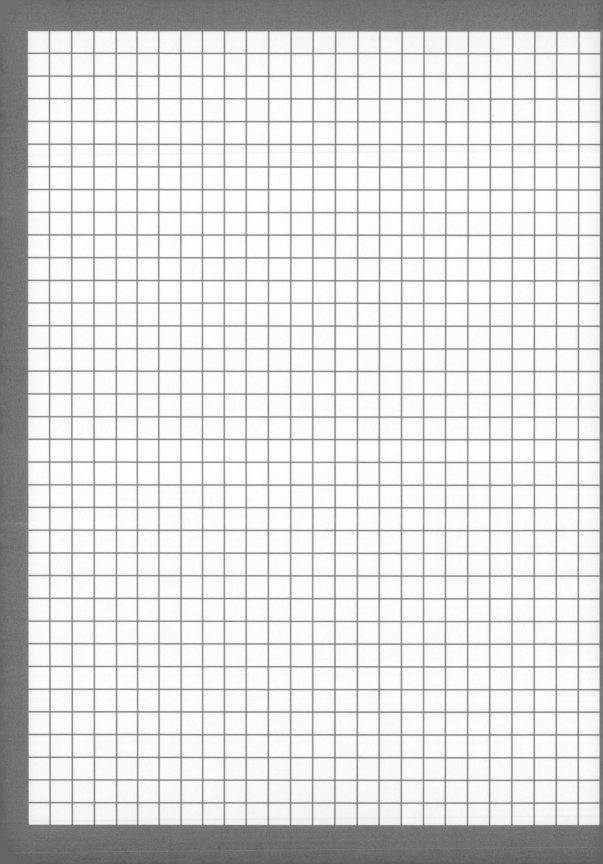

EARLY

It is morning in Tokyo. The streets are silent, except for the quiet whir of the trains and the pin pon, pin pin pon of the city's pedestrian crossings.

In the many dwellings that make up this vast metropolis, locals are settling down to breakfast. Perhaps a traditional meal of ichi-ju-san-sai (one soup, three dishes): a bowl of miso soup filled with tiny clams or nameko mushrooms; fragrant, short-grain rice; and fish, grilled with sake and salt, served with daikon oroshi (grated Japanese radish). There will be sides, such as dashimaki tamago, a succulent rolled omelette made with eggs, soy and dashi; sheets of nori, flash-toasted with some sesame oil; pickles and furikake (rice seasoning), and a single, sour-sweet pickled plum known as umeboshi.

Or maybe it's a bowl of TKG (tamago kake gohan): a raw egg cracked over steaming hot rice, dusted with a smattering of furikake, nori and katsuobushi (dried skipjack tuna flakes). Nattō – sticky, fermented soybeans that are an acquired taste – could be added to the mix.

But not everyone has time to prepare breakfast.

Some make their way to dark, smoky kissaten, the old-school coffee shops, to have 'morning sets' – thickly sliced toast topped with a neat square of butter, served with boiled eggs and strong black coffee.

Some, nursing a hangover or simply after something a little more filling, can be found in ochazuke shops, gingerly sipping the hot tea broth poured over rice and ingredients such as grilled salmon, salmon roe, mentaiko (spicy pollock roe) or sashimi. Others huddle around the counters of ramen-ya (noodle shops), slurping down a bowl of hearty ramen or tsukemen (dipping noodles), a salty, savoury melting pot of umami.

You'll also find locals in cafes or one of the city's many French-influenced bakeries filled with glorious plump buns of the soft, airy, sweet variety. Lured there by the enticing aroma of freshly baked bread, customers gather to pick up sweet pastries, from meron-pan (a melon-shaped sweet bun), kurimu-pan (cream buns) and karēpan (curry buns) to flaky croissants, madeleines, matcha and chocolate scones.

TSUKEMONO
JAPANESE PICKLES

Delicate, nutritious and colourful, tsukemono – 'tsuke' meaning soaked and 'mono' meaning thing – have existed in Japan since ancient times: an essential part of Japan's culinary culture. Depending on the pickling method, the vegetables are enhanced and transformed into lightly crunchy, salty, sweet or tangy versions of their natural selves.

Some pickling methods intensify the vegetables' original colours; ume or plum, pickled with salt and red shiso (perilla) leaves, is imbued with an alluring rosy-pink blush; takuan (daikon/Japanese radish) takes on a vibrant yellow from the dried fruit of gardenias; and beni shōga (ginger) turns a rich red from the umezu (plum vinegar) it is pickled in.

Rich in nutrients, vitamins and probiotics, tsukemono are enjoyed with traditional Japanese meals from breakfast to supper. There are entire restaurants dedicated to tsukemono, and in summer, kyūri asazuke (salt-pickled cucumbers on sticks) can be purchased; an antidote to combat the sticky heat.

Tsukemono often differ from region to region and season to season, so if you love pickles, it is worth purchasing regional specialties that may be hard to find elsewhere. In Tokyo, you can find these in depachika (department store food halls) or in regional satellite stalls and regional fairs. Sealed and beautifully packaged, they are a lingering reminder of Japan when your trip has ended, and can be enjoyed simply with rice and a warming bowl of miso soup, or with rice porridge.

NUKAZUKE
RICE BRAN PICKLES

Nukazuke are vegetables pickled in a nuka (rice bran) paste (nukadoko), and they are quite the personal pickle. The lactic acid–producing colonies crucial to the fermentation process require bacteria from human skin (clean hands) and the environment to get started – which is why nukazuke tastes different from household to household. The paste, or nukadoko, needs to be stirred daily (a good quick mix by hand will do) to aerate it and keep the microbes at bay.

Being a live culture, nukadoko has a yeasty, earthy smell, the scent varying from season to season. With proper care, it can be kept for an extraordinarily long time, with Japanese families often passing down their nukadoko through the generations.

Once established, vegetables can be quick-pickled in nukadoko for a few hours or overnight, with the resulting pickles being crispy, salty, tangy and rich in lactobacillus and vitamin B.

SERVES 4–8 AS A SIDE DISH

500 g (1 lb 2 oz) rice bran

1 × 2 cm (¾ in) piece konbu (dried kelp), soaked in cold water for 15 minutes to rehydrate

1 dried red chilli

125 ml (½ cup) beer or 1 tablespoon sake lees

1 cucumber

100 g (3½ oz) salt, plus extra for salting the cucumber

1 carrot

1 daikon (Japanese radish)

1   In a large, heavy-based frying pan over medium–high heat, toast the rice bran, stirring frequently to prevent it from browning, until fragrant. Set aside to cool.

2   Combine the cooled toasted rice bran, rehydrated konbu and dried chilli in a clean, non-reactive container. Add the beer or sake lees to the mixture, along with enough water to obtain the consistency of wet sand: this is your nukadoko.

3   Rub the cucumber with salt, place it in the nukadoko container and cover with the nukadoko. Without salting them, add the carrot and daikon to the container and cover with the nukadoko. Ensure the walls of the nukadoko container are clean, as any nukadoko on the sides or trapped beneath the lid can foster bad bacteria and destroy the batch. Leave the nukadoko in a cool, dark place for 3 days, giving it a quick, thorough mix with clean hands every day.

4   Nukadoko is best stored between 10–20°C (50–68°F). Between 0–10°C (32–50°F) it is under-active or inactive, and when stored above 20°C (68°F) it is too active and will turn sour quickly. Any white bacteria that forms as a layer on top of the nukadoko is harmless and can be mixed back in.

5 After 3 days, the vegetables should taste slightly pickled. Continue adding and removing the vegetables as desired, topping up with more toasted rice bran and salt in a 10:1 ratio if the nukadoko gets too watery. As the nukadoko matures, you will find that the vegetables pickle faster.

6 To serve the nukazuke, brush the excess bran from the vegetables, rinse well, dry and slice to serve.

7 If you are not using the nukadoko for a while, it can be kept in the fridge or freezer to slow or stop activity respectively.

Note
If the nukadoko starts to smell sour or unpleasant, rather than yeasty or earthy, or if it begins to grow mould, it should be discarded.

SUNOMONO
RICE VINEGAR PICKLES

Sunomono are brined in Japanese rice vinegar, which gives the pickles a crunchy texture and a sweet and tangy taste. Rice vinegar has a low acidity, so the pickles must be stored in the fridge.

**MAKES A 1 LITRE (1 QT)
JAR OF PICKLES**

150 ml (5 fl oz) rice vinegar

75 g (2¾ oz) caster (superfine) sugar

1¾ teaspoons salt

a selection of vegetables, such as radish, turnip, daikon (Japanese radish), pickling onion, sliced

1 dried red chilli

1 In a saucepan over medium heat, bring the rice vinegar, sugar, salt and 250 ml (1 cup) of water to the boil. Remove from the heat and cool to room temperature. Transfer to a sterilised 1 litre (1 qt) glass jar with a lid and refrigerate until chilled.

2 Place the vegetables and the dried chilli in the pickling liquid, keeping them submerged in the liquid with a freezer sheet or a piece of plastic wrap. Leave to cure in the fridge for 1 week; the pickles will keep for 1 week after that.

PICKLES
< ピクルス >

1p … ¥756

3p … ¥2,100

※鮮度ÿ·ソース系と組み合せ
ても OK!! (+100円)

お出汁のピクルス
和える酢
¥756

TSUKUDANI
BRAISED KONBU

The Japanese philosophy of mottainai or 'do not waste' is embraced in this dish, which turns konbu (dried kelp) left over from the dashi-making process into a delicious, intensely salty-sweet pickle that can be enjoyed with rice or as a snack with green tea.

SERVES 2 AS A SNACK

15 × 2 cm (¾ in) squares cooked konbu (dried kelp) left over from making Katsuo dashi (page 220; see note)

2 whole dried shiitake mushrooms, rehydrated in warm water and thinly sliced

100 ml (3½ fl oz) soy sauce

100 ml (3½ fl oz) sake

50 g (1¾ oz) caster (superfine) sugar

1 Place all the ingredients in a heavy-based saucepan, along with enough water to cover them. Cut out a circle of baking paper the same size as the mouth of the saucepan and place on top of the liquid; this will prevent it from evaporating too quickly. Cook over very low heat for 1–2 hours, or until the konbu has softened, topping up with a small amount of water if the liquid boils dry. Drain and allow to cool before serving.

2 Tsukudani can be kept in the fridge for up to 3 months.

Note
If you don't have cooked konbu left over from making dashi, rehydrate 15 × 2 cm (¾ in) squares of dried konbu in cold water for 15 minutes, drain, then proceed with the rest of the recipe.

GARI
PICKLED GINGER

Gari is most commonly found in neat little mounds on a plate of sashimi, eaten as a palate cleanser in between the different cuts of fish.

MAKES 250 G (9 OZ)

200 ml (6¾ fl oz) rice vinegar

25 g (1 oz) caster (superfine) sugar

250 g (9 oz) young ginger, peeled

1 Combine the rice vinegar and sugar in a saucepan and cook over medium heat until the sugar dissolves. Remove from the heat and cool.

2 Using a mandoline, slice the ginger very finely and salt well. Leave for 15 minutes, then rinse and drain. Squeeze the excess moisture out of the ginger, then transfer to a sterile container or sterilised glass jar with a lid. Pour the rice vinegar mixture over the ginger and seal.

3 Place in the fridge to pickle for a minimum of 3 days before using. The gari will keep in the fridge for up to 3 months.

ICHI-JU-SAN-SAI

One soup, three dishes.
A tenet of Japanese cuisine and the
foundation of Japanese breakfast.

Dressed in yukata, the Japanese cotton robe,
we take a seat on zabuton (floor cushions) on
the tatami mat floor as our room attendant,
attired in a beautiful silk kimono and matching
obi, hands us a warm oshibori (towel) and a cup
of fragrant green tea with puffed rice.

'Shitsurei itashimasu,' she murmurs as she
places small plate after small plate on the
gleaming lacquered tray in front of us.
An owan of hot miso soup, its steam rising

in spiral wafts when we remove the lid; a single umeboshi plum; an assortment of pickles and furikake; a bowl of freshly made yudōfu (tofu) sitting in a broth of soy milk; some perfectly rolled Japanese omelette; and a small grill to toast the seaweed and grill the fish. It is a feast for the senses: the saltiness of the rice toppings, the sourness from the pickles and plum, the sweetness of the rice, the umami from the miso, the delicate little vessels.

We hear her shuffling softly across the tatami mat on the other side of the shōji screen as we dine, wrapping up our futon. Then she returns, presenting us with perfect halves of a grapefruit set in a beautiful glass bowl and hōjicha, roasted green tea, to finish.

'Goyukkuri dōzo,' she says with a smile – take your time – and kneels, gives a genteel bow and excuses herself.

We are in a traditional Japanese inn, or ryokan, in Hakone, near Mount Fuji, and this is Japanese breakfast.

It is the secret to Japanese health and longevity: a diet of whole grains, tofu, fish, vegetables and fermented foods, prepared according to the philosophy of 'hara hachi bu' (eat until you are 80 per cent full, hence the tiny little plates).

In theory, at least.

Realistically, a good ryokan – a visit to Japan would not be complete without a stay in one – will leave you so full you resort to somewhat unbecoming actions such as rolling off your zabuton or kotatsu (a simply blissful heated dining table with blanket) from being overfed.

At one ryokan in Kyoto, we resorted to shuffling around in circles in the small room to work off the first few courses before we could attempt to fit more in.

For those who don't get the chance to take on the full majesty of a ryokan-style Japanese breakfast, a more restrained version called asacha (morning tea) can be found at Yakumo Saryo, in the Tokyo neighbourhood of Meguro.

The creation of Shinichiro Ogata, designer of the Andaz Tokyo and Japan's Aēsop boutiques, Yakumo Saryo was designed as an escape from the clamour of Tokyo. Laid out as a traditional Japanese home – albeit entirely reimagined – it is nestled among lush greenery at the top of a dramatic flight of stone steps, shielded from view by an imposing white noren bearing the restaurant's simple, striking crest.

Breakfast is served in the Sabo teahouse, at a large table with a view of the trees. It starts with tea: vibrant flecks of yellow chrysanthemum petals floating among the deep green stems and leaves in a delicate glass teapot, followed by a fragrant hōjicha, freshly roasted.

Asacha, the traditional rendition of ichi-ju-san-sai follows, with a particular focus on pickles, before we are presented with a selection of modern wagashi (Japanese sweets) in unexpected flavours such as peanut, kōji (fermented rice) and sake, paired with a bowl of frothy, bittersweet matcha to finish.

It's all very calm, very light and very Zen – which is a good thing, for it is a communal table, and the other diners might be a little bewildered by a food-induced calisthenics display.

Clockwise from top left: Japanese pickles (pages 18–25), Miso soup (page 29), steamed rice, Salt-grilled salmon (page 28), Rolled egg omelette (page 32) and Sauteed root vegetables (page 79).

SHIOZAKE
SALT-GRILLED SALMON

In ancient Japan, fish was preserved by a salting and drying process called himono, which dates back to the Nara period (710–794), when records show fish being presented in this manner to the emperor and the gods. Today, himono is less heavily salted, the salt used to enhance the flavour of the fish, rather than as a preservation method.

Shiozake – 'shio' meaning salt and 'zake' meaning salmon – is one of the most common types of salted fish sold in Japanese supermarkets. You'll find it in a traditional Japanese breakfast, in bentō, as a humble onigiri (rice ball) topping or filling, or with ikura (salmon roe) on rice. We like to grill it over binchotan (Japanese charcoal), but if you don't have a charcoal grill at home, you can grill (broil) it in your oven using the grill (broiler) setting with the skin-side up or pan-fry the fish as per the method below.

SERVES 4

4 × 200 g (7 oz) salmon fillets, skin on, scaled and pin-boned

1 tablespoon sake

72 g (¼ cup) salt

1 tablespoon neutral oil, for frying

1   Dry the salmon thoroughly with paper towels. Pour the sake over the fillets, then sprinkle each one with 1 tablespoon of salt. Line a large plate with paper towels to absorb excess liquid, and place the fillets on top. Place the fish in the fridge, uncovered, for 5–7 hours to dry out and concentrate the flavours.

2   Before cooking, rinse the excess salt off the fillets and pat them dry. Heat the oil in a frying pan over medium–high heat. Cook the fillets skin-side down for 4–5 minutes, depending on their thickness, until the skin is crisp or dark brown in spots. Turn and cook for a further 3–4 minutes, until the salmon flakes easily when tested with a fork, and is still a little pink in the centre.

MISOSHIRU

MISO SOUP

When not in Japan, we always miss the miso soups, which differ from region to region and season to season. They can be light, thick and sweet, simply adorned with a lightly boiled Kyoto carrot. Or they can be a deep, dark reddish-brown, briny and smoky, accentuated with just a few stems of mizuna (Japanese mustard greens). They are almost always served in a lidded bowl to keep the scent in, so that it gently fills the air around you when you lift the lid.

Miso soup is as much about the blend of miso used as it is the dashi that forms its base. The recipe here is for the most common type of miso soup, a blend of red and white miso.

SERVES 8

2 litres (2 qts) cold
   Katsuo dashi (page 220)
90 g (⅓ cup) shiromiso
   (white miso paste)
70 g (2½ oz) akamiso
   (red miso paste)
soy sauce, to taste

Per person you will need:

1 tablespoon diced silken tofu
1 teaspoon finely sliced
   spring onion (scallion)

1   Place the katsuo dashi in a large saucepan. Place the shiromiso and akamiso in a fine strainer, and immerse the strainer in the dashi. Using a whisk, whisk and press the miso through the strainer and into the dashi. Discard any solids left in the strainer and season the soup with soy sauce to taste.

2   When ready to serve, place the tofu and spring onion in individual bowls. Over low heat, bring the miso soup to just below boiling (see notes). Stir to combine the dashi and miso, then ladle into the bowls.

Notes
Allowing the miso to boil affects the taste and texture of the finished product. It should be heated to just below boiling, or else it will become grainy.
   Make sure that you stir your miso soup before drinking it, so the miso and dashi flavours are combined.

DASHIMAKI TAMAGO

ROLLED EGG OMELETTE

Dashimaki tamago is the Japanese version of an omelette, with delicate, thin layers of egg folded over each other to form a roll. Part of a traditional Japanese breakfast, it can also be found adorning nigiri sushi, in temaki (hand rolls), and filled with unagi (freshwater eel) in unagi restaurants. Dashimaki tamago also makes a delicious addition to bentō.

This was the recipe we used at our Japanese restaurant, chotto, and is on the savoury side. The dashi gives the omelette a lovely juiciness and, if you like, you can also add freshly chopped herbs. We use a rectangular copper pan specially made for dashimaki tamago that can be purchased in Japan or online, but the omelette can also be made in a normal frying pan.

MAKES 1 ROLL

4 eggs
100 ml (3½ fl oz) Katsuo dashi or Konbu dashi (pages 220–221)
1 teaspoon soy sauce
1 teaspoon mirin
1 tablespoon sake
1 teaspoon potato starch
neutral oil, for frying

1   In a bowl, beat together all the ingredients, except the oil, then strain into a second bowl. Heat a dashimaki tamago pan (also known as a tamagoyaki pan) or a frying pan over medium heat. Using chopsticks or tongs, dip a small piece of paper towel into the oil and use it to coat the base and sides of the pan well. Keeping the pan well-oiled will prevent the omelette from sticking.

2   Pour one-quarter of the egg mixture into the pan, tilting it so that the entire surface is covered. When the egg is almost set, use chopsticks or a spatula to roll up the omelette from the back of the pan towards you. Once the omelette is rolled, push it to the back of the pan.

3   Pour in another quarter of the egg mixture, lifting the rolled omelette slightly to let the egg flow underneath, and tilting the pan to coat the entire surface once again. Roll the omelette as above. Repeat the pouring and rolling process twice more with the remaining egg mixture.

4   Turn the rolled omelette out onto a piece of plastic wrap, then use a sushi mat to press into a rectangular shape.

KITSUNE UDON

The story goes that the legendary kitsune (fox guardians) of the Inari shrine love fried tofu, which is how this dish of udon noodle soup topped with two pockets of deep-fried tofu – one for each of the fox guardians – came to be called kitsune udon.

First invented in the Meiji era (1868–1912), kitsune udon is a simple, comforting dish in which the quality of the dashi really shines through. Wakame (sea mustard) and aburaage (deep-fried tofu pockets) are the only toppings, but they soak up the flavour of the stock and are an absolute treat.

In this recipe, we show you how you can make your own udon. Good udon can also be found in the frozen section of Asian and Japanese supermarkets.

SERVES 1

150 g (5½ oz) fresh
  Udon (below)

250 ml (1 cup) Katsuo dashi
  or Konbu dashi (pages 220–221)

1 tablespoon soy sauce

1 tablespoon sake

1 tablespoon wakame
  (sea mustard; see glossary),
  rehydrated if dried

Shichimi tōgarashi (page 227),
  to serve (optional)

Udon

200 g (1⅓ cups) plain
  (all-purpose) flour

1 teaspoon salt

potato starch, to dust

Simmered aburaage

4 pieces aburaage
  (deep-fried tofu;
  see glossary)

60 ml (¼ cup) soy sauce

2 tablespoons sake

2 tablespoons mirin

1 tablespoon caster
  (superfine) sugar

1   To make the udon, combine the flour and salt in a bowl and add 100 ml (3½ fl oz) of water, one-third at a time, mixing well after each addition. Knead the dough until it forms a smooth ball, about 5 minutes. Wrap the dough with plastic wrap and set aside to rest for 30 minutes.

2   Press the dough into a rectangular shape, then roll it out into a square approximately 5 mm (¼ in) thick and dust all over with potato starch. Fold the dough into thirds, as though you were folding a letter for mailing, and use a sharp knife to cut into noodles 5 mm (¼ in) wide. Dust again with potato starch to prevent the udon from sticking together. Cover with plastic wrap and refrigerate if not cooking immediately.

3   To make the simmered aburaage, bring a saucepan of water to the boil over high heat. Boil the aburaage pieces for 1–2 minutes to remove any excess oil, then drain and rinse in cold water. Squeeze the excess water out of the aburaage, then cut each piece in half.

4   Combine the remaining ingredients in a clean saucepan, along with 250 ml (1 cup) of water. Add the halved aburaage and more water to cover, if necessary. Bring to the boil over medium heat, then reduce the heat to low and simmer for 10 minutes. Reserve two pieces of simmered aburaage for this recipe and transfer the remaining pieces to an airtight container. The left-over aburaage will keep in the fridge for 3 days.

5   To assemble the kitsune udon, warm the dashi in a saucepan over low heat and add the soy sauce and sake. Season to taste with salt.

6   Bring a large saucepan of water to the boil over high heat and cook the udon for 4 minutes (or follow the packet instructions if you are using store-bought noodles). Drain well.

7   To serve, place the udon in a bowl and pour over the dashi. Top with the simmered aburaage pieces and wakame, and sprinkle with shichimi tōgarashi (if using).

EARLY

YŌSHOKU

Japan's take on Western cuisine. 'Retro' Western dishes that the Japanese have made their own.

Today, we are on a yōshoku quest: a dawn-to-dust exploration of a cuisine that has influenced the city's culinary scene since the Meiji era (1868–1912).

9:00
Location: Hotel Okura, Toranomon

Only three dishes are served for breakfast at Nouvelle Epoque in the revered Hotel Okura, one of these being their famous French toast, which comes with a medley of seasonal fresh fruits, a small pitcher of maple syrup and a stick of butter.

French toast at The Okura is a luxury, but it is the epitome of its kind: a perfect, plump, glistening and golden rectangle, crisp on the outside and beautifully fluffy and light on the inside, with just the right amount of sweetness and saltiness from the maple syrup and butter.

If you aren't staying at the hotel, dining is a wonderful way to glimpse this Japanese design icon envisioned by one of the 20th century's leading architects, Yoshirō Taniguchi. Established in 1962 for the 1964 Tokyo Olympics, The Okura underwent a three-year reconstruction in 2016, with Taniguchi's son, Yoshio Taniguchi, leading The Okura's new design aesthetic. The distinctly recognisable Okura lanterns have been retained, alongside the many other motifs of Japanese tradition and beauty.

11:30
Location: Shiseido Parlour, Ginza

One of the poshest yōshoku establishments, Shiseido Parlour in Ginza was established in 1902 as a soda fountain and ice cream shop within the first Shiseido beauty store. It became a yōshoku restaurant in 1928, and is now an eleven-floor building on the site where Shiseido was founded.

On floor 4.5 is the Shiseido Parlour Restaurant, a stately, cream-toned space with a menu that steps back in time to perfectly honed yōshoku classics from the Meiji to Shōwa (1926–1989) eras. Start with a consomme soup or meat croquettes, then choose between curry rice, hayashi rice (beef in a demi-glace sauce, served with steamed rice), macaroni au gratin, omuraisu (omelette rice) or Japanese-style pilaf.

One floor below is the iconic scarlet-hued Salon de Café. An ojō-sama's (noble young lady's) dream, it once offered delicate cakes presented for selection on polished silver platters, and pretty strawberry parfaits that were savoured by the stylish Ginza set since the early 1900s. Though the cake service is no longer, you can still find classic kissa-fare, from pudding à la mode to sherbert, and strawberry and chocolate parfaits. If you are after crepes suzette and cakes, however, you might like to try the Kobe-founded Henri Charpentier, which is also located in Ginza.

15:00
Location: Kayaba Coffee, Yanaka
....

As Japan continues to modernise, jun-kissa (pure kissatens, or old-school coffee shops) are slowly vanishing, future generations deciding not to take the family business on. In some regional areas, younger folk are moving back to their hometowns to take over their family (or sometimes non-family) kissatens, but not all establishments are as fortunate, Angelus in Asakusa among the closed set.

One of the jun-kissa saved from this fate is Kayaba Coffee in Yanaka. Established in 1938, the kissa is nestled within a handsome 1916-era house on the corner of Yanaka's Kototoi-dori, its iconic yellow sign a beacon for locals and visitors alike. Its 68-year run faced an uncertain future when the owner passed away in 2006, but it was rescued three years later by the owners of nearby SCAI the Bathhouse and a local not-for-profit group.

Set in a tranquil part of the city, Kayaba is worth a visit if you have the time. You'll still find the yellow sign and the building's historic features: the retro door, the patinaed floors, the rich, gleaming wooden ceiling panels, frosted glass windows and dim retro lights. We settle into one of the terracotta-hued cushy leather chairs on the ground floor – the second is laid with tatami mats – and order coffee floats and purin (creme caramel, this one topped with candied walnuts), watching guests read books, sip on melon floats and nibble on egg sando.

18:00
Location: Delifucious, Toranomon
....

After a day of classics, we are ready for one of the most exciting yōshoku establishments on the scene, a creation by young chef Shinya Kudo, who blends his decade-long traditional Japanese training at prestigious sushi-ya (sushi restaurants) with the most unlikely companions: burgers and hot dogs.

Delifucious offers diners a choice of fish fillets sourced from the famed Toyosu fish market, either breaded and fried or charcoal-grilled traditional-style with saikyo miso, then nestled in a hot dog bun brushed with tofu-based sauce. We opt for the tempura anago (saltwater eel) and dashimaki tamago (rolled egg omelette) hot dogs, and a kani korokke (crab croquette) burger with a dollop of kanimiso.

21:00
Location: Hoshino Coffee, Shimokitazawa
....

We're meeting a Japanese friend who can't drink, and since that rules out a bar, we've decided to meet at her local kissaten, Hoshino Coffee, which has branches throughout Tokyo. It's surprisingly popular late into the night, with young and old Tokyoites meeting up in the dark, cosy interior for some hand-dripped coffee, frothy royal milk tea, and dessert in the form of impossibly fluffy souffle hotcakes (which come with the tiniest pitcher of maple syrup) and French toast with chestnuts and chestnut cream.

DORAYAKI
RED BEAN PANCAKES

Dorayaki is a traditional Japanese confection: sweet red bean paste sandwiched between two grilled pancakes. Originally, dorayaki consisted of one pancake that was folded into a semi-circle around the red bean paste; the dorayaki we know today was invented by Usagiya in the historic district of Ueno in 1914.

'Dora' means gong and 'yaki' means grill, and legend goes that the name came about after a farmer cooked pancakes over a gong left behind by a samurai, Benkei, who sought refuge in his home.

Today, dorayaki is filled with less traditional fillings such as cream, custard, matcha, chocolate and chestnut cream. There is also a National Dorayaki Day on the 4th of April.

SERVES 4

2 eggs

50 g (1¾ oz) caster (superfine) sugar

100 g (⅔ cup) plain (all-purpose) flour

2 teaspoons baking powder

1 teaspoon baking soda

neutral oil, for frying

Red bean paste (page 143), to serve

100 ml (3½ fl oz) cream, whipped to stiff peaks, to serve

1   Bring a large saucepan of water to a simmer over medium heat. In a heatproof bowl large enough to fit over the saucepan without touching the water's surface, mix the eggs and sugar. Place the bowl over the simmering water and whisk the egg mixture until thick. Remove from the heat.

2   Sift the flour and baking powder into the egg mixture and mix until just combined. Stir the baking soda into 80 ml (⅓ cup) of water and fold into the batter, taking care not to overmix, or else the pancakes will end up tough.

3   Lightly oil a large, non-stick frying pan (or a dorayaki pan if you have one) and place over medium heat. Pour the dorayaki batter into the pan to make pancakes roughly 8 cm (3 in) in diameter and cook, turning once when large holes form on the surface of the pancakes, until both sides are golden brown. Transfer to a plate and allow to cool to room temperature.

4   Spread a pancake with red bean paste and top with a spoonful of whipped cream. Sandwich with a second pancake and repeat until the remaining pancakes and filling have been used.

FRENCH TOAST

This recipe is inspired by the French toast at Hotel Okura's La Belle Epoque ('now Nouvelle Epoque'), which is hailed as Tokyo's finest. The bread needs to be soaked in the egg mixture for at least 12 hours, so it's best prepared one day in advance. The resulting French toast is wonderfully crisp and golden on the outside, with just the right amount of fluffy, eggy softness within.

SERVES 4

200 ml (6¾ fl oz) milk

50 g (1¾ oz) caster (superfine) sugar

4 eggs

½ teaspoon vanilla bean paste

4 slices stale white bread, approximately 3 cm (1¼ in) thick, crusts removed

1 tablespoon unsalted butter, for frying, plus extra to serve

fruit and maple syrup, to serve

1   Place the milk and sugar in a small saucepan over low heat and stir until the sugar dissolves. Remove from the heat and transfer to the fridge.

2   Once the milk mixture has cooled, add the eggs and vanilla bean paste and blend until well combined. Slice the bread in half lengthways and place on the bottom of a dish or container in a single layer. Pour the egg mixture over the bread, ensuring all pieces are equally immersed, and transfer to the fridge to soak for 12–24 hours. Halfway through the refrigeration time, use a spatula to turn the pieces over, taking care as the bread will be very soft.

3   Before cooking, carefully remove the bread from the egg mixture and place on a cake rack over a tray to drain well. In a large non-stick frying pan with a lid, melt the butter over medium heat, ensuring the entire surface of the pan is coated. Add the bread, reduce the heat to low, cover and cook for 3–5 minutes. Turn the French toast with a spatula, cover again and continue cooking for another 3–5 minutes, or until the centre of the bread is hot and both sides are golden brown and crisp.

4   Transfer the French toast to a warm plate and serve with seasonal fruit, maple syrup and butter.

YUZU MADELEINES

French and French–Japanese patisseries are bountiful in Tokyo, with one of our favourite sweet treats being yuzu madeleines: soft, eggy and fluffy cakes filled with a tart yuzu curd. While quick to make, the batter does need at least two hours to chill, so is best prepared in advance.

MAKES 12

90 g (3 oz) unsalted butter, plus extra for greasing

2 teaspoons honey

2 eggs

80 g (⅓ cup) caster (superfine) sugar

½ teaspoon vanilla bean paste

pinch of salt

zest of 1 yuzu (see glossary) or lemon

90 g (3 oz) plain (all-purpose) flour

½ teaspoon baking powder

Yuzu curd

40 ml (1¼ fl oz) yuzu juice

40 g (1½ oz) caster (superfine) sugar

45 g (1½ oz) unsalted butter

2 egg yolks

1   Fill a large bowl with cold water. In a small saucepan, preferably one with a light-coloured bottom, melt the butter over low heat. As the butter begins to foam, swirl the pan so it cooks evenly. Continue to cook the melted butter until it turns from golden brown to nut brown, then remove from the heat. Place the base of the pan in the bowl of cold water to immediately stop the butter browning further.

2   Allow the browned butter to cool to room temperature, then add the honey and stir to combine well. Strain the mixture into a bowl to remove any dark sediment, then set aside.

3   Place the eggs and sugar in the bowl of an electric mixer and beat until pale and fluffy. Add the vanilla bean paste, salt and zest and beat well. Mix in the flour and baking powder until just combined, then stir in the browned butter mixture. Cover with plastic wrap and transfer to the fridge for 2 hours or overnight.

4   Meanwhile, make the yuzu curd. Place the yuzu juice, sugar and butter in a saucepan over low heat and bring to a simmer to dissolve the sugar. Place the egg yolks in a bowl and slowly add the yuzu mixture in a thin stream, whisking continuously to prevent curdling. Return the mixture to the pan and cook over low heat, stirring constantly, until it thickens and can coat the back of a spoon. Transfer to a container, press a sheet of plastic wrap on top to prevent a skin from forming, and refrigerate until cold.

5   To bake the madeleines, preheat the oven to 180°C (350°F) and grease a madeleine tin with a little bit of butter. Pour the batter into the tin, filling each hole only two-thirds of the way. Bake in the preheated oven for 7 minutes, or until golden brown and a skewer inserted into the centre of a madeleine comes out clean. Allow the madeleines to cool before removing them from the tin.

6   Serve with the yuzu curd.

Almond Croissant

DKA
Dominique's Kouign Amann

350

MATCHA FINANCIERS

Another French pastry much loved by the Japanese, financiers can be found in bakeries all over Tokyo in flavours of butter and matcha. These financiers are quick to bake, but the mixture needs to be rested in the fridge for at least two hours.

MAKES 6

35 g (1¼ oz) unsalted butter, plus extra for greasing

10 g (¼ oz) plain (all-purpose) flour

13 g (½ oz) almond flour

3 g (¹⁄₁₀ oz) matcha (green tea powder)

40 g (1½ oz) egg white (approximately 1 egg)

30 g (1 oz) caster (superfine) sugar

10 g (¼ oz) honey

1   Fill a large bowl with cold water. In a small saucepan, preferably one with a light-coloured bottom, melt the butter over low heat. As the butter begins to foam, swirl the pan so it cooks evenly. Continue to cook the melted butter until it turns from golden brown to nut brown, then remove from the heat. Place the base of the pan in the bowl of cold water to immediately stop the butter browning further. Strain the browned butter into a bowl to remove any dark sediment, then set aside to cool to room temperature.

2   Sift the flour, almond flour and matcha together three times. In a large bowl, whisk the egg white and sugar together. Add the dry mixture and whisk to combine, then stir in the browned butter and honey.

3   Cover the financier batter with plastic wrap and transfer to the fridge for 2 hours or overnight.

4   Preheat the oven to 180°C (350°F) and grease a financier tin with a little bit of butter. Pour the refrigerated batter into the holes of the tin and bake for 12 minutes, or until golden brown and a skewer inserted into the centre of a financier comes out clean. Allow the financiers to cool before removing them from the tin.

FUNWARI HOTTOKEKI

SOUFFLE HOTCAKES

Japan's souffle hotcakes have a reputation for being incredibly popular and incredibly fuwa fuwa (fluffy).

At renowned kissaten (coffee shop) chain Hoshino Coffee, they are served late into the night with whipped butter and a choice of black sugar, maple syrup or honey. Strawberries and cream and matcha, served in summer, and mont blanc with chestnut, served in autumn, are just some of the other flavours these fuwa fuwa hotcakes come in.

If making a single large hotcake with this recipe, you will need a 16 cm (6 in) metal cake ring, which you can find in baking stores.

SERVES 2

30 g (1 oz) plain
  (all-purpose) flour

¾ teaspoon baking powder

2 eggs, separated

1 tablespoon milk

20 g (¾ oz) caster
  (superfine) sugar

neutral oil, for greasing

maple syrup, cream or fruit,
  to serve

1   To make the hotcake batter, sift the flour and baking powder into a large mixing bowl and whisk to combine. In a separate bowl, beat the egg yolks and milk together, then fold into the dry ingredients until just combined.

2   Just before cooking, beat the egg whites and sugar together in a clean, dry bowl until stiff peaks form. Fold into the hotcake base, taking care not to overmix.

3   To make one large hotcake, preheat the oven to 180°C (350°F) and grease and line a 16 cm (6 in) metal cake ring with baking paper. Grease a medium oven-safe non-stick frying pan, place the cake ring in the centre and heat over medium heat until a drop of cold water placed in the pan sizzles, but doesn't evaporate immediately. Pour the hotcake batter into the cake ring and transfer the pan to the preheated oven for approximately 15 minutes, or until a skewer inserted into the centre of the hotcake comes out clean.

4   Remove the hotcake from the oven and, using a pair of tongs, carefully remove the cake ring and baking paper. Place the frying pan back on the stovetop over medium heat. Carefully flip the hotcake and cook until the other side is golden brown.

5   To make four small hotcakes, grease a large non-stick frying pan and heat over medium heat until a drop of cold water placed in the pan sizzles, but doesn't evaporate immediately. Place four even mounds of batter in the pan and reduce the heat to low. Using the back of a ladle, shape the mounds into circles. Cook for approximately 5 minutes, or until a skewer inserted into the centre of a hotcake comes out clean, then turn and cook for a further 5 minutes, or until both sides are golden brown.

6   Serve immediately, accompanied by your choice of toppings and condiments.

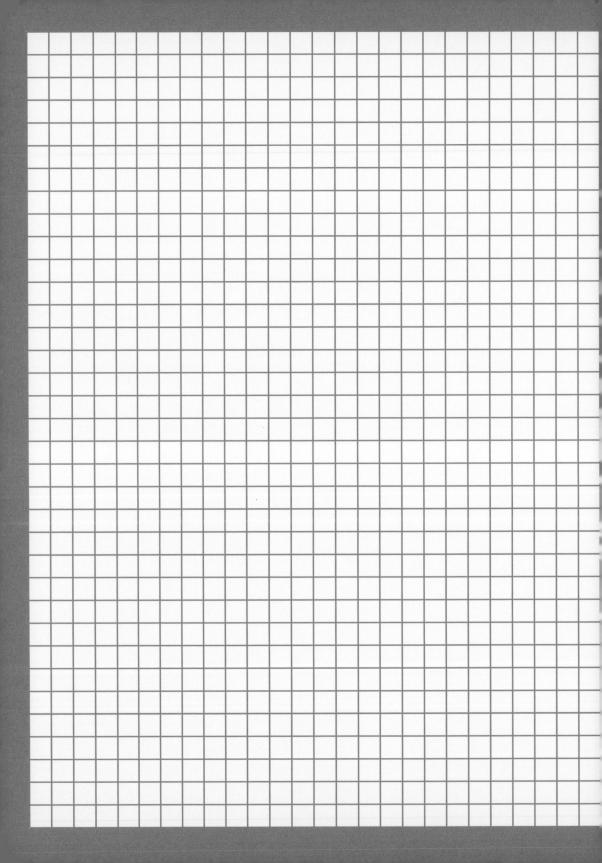

MID

Midday in Tokyo. The city transforms into a permanent Shibuya crossing. In the skyscraper districts of Marunochi and Shinjuku, salarymen and office ladies pour out of their high-rise office towers, heading for their favourite ramen shops, curry houses and depachika.

Depachika – 'depa' being short for department store and 'chika' meaning basement – are veritable treasure troves, and the most renowned are within the city's eminent department stores – Isetan, Takashimaya and Daimaru.

There's a grocer, with prized musk melons, apples, peaches and other perfect fruit, wrapped in tissue or silk and nestled carefully in paulownia-wood boxes. There's a fishmonger, where gleaming slabs of tuna and roe are displayed alongside seasonal delicacies such as shirako (sperm sac) or hamo (eel). There are specialty pickle stores, umeboshi (pickled plum) stores, and stores selling furikake (rice seasoning).

There's a cellar, filled with bottles of rare and exquisite French wine, prized whiskey and magnums of sake, staffed by sommeliers. There are tea shops established centuries ago, filled with canisters of precious gyokuro, matcha and teas from the regions of Uji and Shizuoka.

Patisseries from notable houses such as Pierre Hermé, Henri Charpentier, Ladurée and Fauchon gleam like jewels in glass cases. Traditional Japanese sweets – soft pillows of mochi, daifuku and wagashi in the shapes of cranes and flowers – shine against black lacquered backdrops. There's always a shop selling baumkuchen, a beloved cake of German origin, the many layers of which resemble the growth rings of a tree – hence its name, which means 'tree cake'.

But at lunch, Tokyoites come for the food stalls, which sell myriad bentō, from humble ¥1000 options to more decadent boxes featuring seafood from Hokkaido or strips of succulent beef from Kobe. There's temarizushi (round rice balls with different toppings), tonkatsu, tempura and sozai (side dishes), all neatly packed to enjoy on the rooftop gardens of the department stores (eating on the streets of Japan is not the done thing).

Lunch, for the salarymen at least, is often a quick affair: a bowl of soba, udon or ramen noodles hastily slurped down; a one-dish donburi (rice topped with sashimi, or simmered or fried meats); or katsu-sando, crumbed and fried pork or beef cutlets sandwiched between fluffy white bread.

Some venture to the konbini, the incredible convenience stores found on every block of the city, which are filled with affordable snacks, from onigiri (rice balls) to yakisoba pan – a uniquely Japanese invention of bread stuffed with fried noodles.

The ladies tend to take lunch a little more leisurely. The areas of Aoyama and Omotesando are dotted with chic cafes situated next to luxury boutiques, where menus feature ladies' lunch sets, potage, salads, Japanese–Italian dishes such as mentaiko pasta (pasta with spicy pollock roe) and uni pasta (pasta with sea urchin), sandwiches, baguettes and cakes.

OYAKODON

Oyakodon is a donburi (rice bowl) containing both chicken and egg, hence the name, which means 'parent and child'. The dish was created in 1891 by the wife of the fifth-generation owner of Tamahide, in the Ningyōchō district of Tokyo.

Oyakodon is quite simple – bite-sized pieces of juicy chicken cooked with slivers of onion and a softly set egg – yet it has a comforting, rich and nostalgic flavour. The key is to scramble the eggs only until they are nearly done, letting the bed of hot rice they sit on cook them just that little bit more. You can make oyakodon in one large frying pan or in four small pans for individual serves.

SERVES 4

4 boneless chicken thighs, skin on, cut into bite-sized pieces

1 tablespoon soy sauce

2 tablespoons sake

2 tablespoons mirin

1 tablespoon neutral oil, for frying

1 onion, finely sliced

200 ml (6¾ fl oz) Katsuo dashi (page 220)

40 g (1½ oz) caster (superfine) sugar

80 ml (⅓ cup) soy sauce

80 ml (⅓ cup) mirin

8 eggs

rice, to serve

2 spring onions (scallions), finely sliced

1   In a large, non-reactive bowl, combine the chicken, soy sauce, sake and mirin and place in the fridge for 15 minutes to marinate.

2   Remove the thighs from the marinade and drain off any excess. In a large frying pan with a lid, heat the oil over medium-high heat and fry the chicken until well browned and cooked through, taking care not to overcrowd the pan. Remove from the pan and set aside.

3   In the same frying pan, fry the onion until softened. Add the katsuo dashi, sugar, soy sauce and mirin and bring to the boil.

4   Whisk the eggs together in a large bowl, then add to the onion mixture. Reduce the heat to medium and gently scramble. When the eggs begin to set, return the chicken to the pan and cover with a lid. Cook for 2 minutes, or until the eggs are mostly set. Serve on top of hot rice and garnish with the spring onion.

JAGAIMO SOBORO DON

MINCE STIR-FRY WITH POTATOES

Soboro, or minced (ground) chicken, is a staple of Japanese home cooking. Traditionally, it is served sanshoku (three colours) style: a vivid yellow from the scrambled eggs, a pop of green from the peas and brown from the soy-cooked chicken itself.

Here, we've left out the peas but added potato, or jagaimo, instead. Soboro can also be used as a filling for onigiri (rice balls) and as a side dish in bentō.

SERVES 4

400 g (14 oz) potatoes, peeled

1 tablespoon salt, plus extra to taste

neutral oil, for frying

300 g (10½ oz) minced (ground) chicken or pork

100 ml (3½ fl oz) Katsuo dashi (page 220), stock or water

2 tablespoons mirin

2 tablespoons light soy sauce

1 teaspoon kuzu (arrowroot) starch or potato starch

4 eggs, beaten

rice, to serve

1 bunch spring onions (scallions), finely sliced

1   Cut the potatoes into bite-sized pieces and rinse under cold water to wash off the starch.

2   Fill a large saucepan with water and add the potato and salt. Bring to the boil and cook until tender, then drain in a colander.

3   Heat a little oil in a large frying pan over high heat and fry the potato until golden brown. Remove from the heat and transfer to a plate lined with paper towels to absorb excess oil.

4   In a clean large frying pan, heat some more oil over high heat and fry the mince until completely cooked and well coloured, using a wooden spoon or spatula to break apart clumps. Remove from the pan and drain, then set aside.

5   In the same frying pan over medium heat, combine the katsuo dashi, mirin and soy sauce. Season with salt to taste and bring to the boil. In a small bowl, mix the starch with enough water to make a very thin paste and add to the boiling liquid to thicken. Stir to combine well, then add the drained mince and potato. Cook until everything is heated through.

6   Meanwhile, heat a little oil in a non-stick frying pan and scramble the eggs until the curds can be broken up into pieces about the same size as the mince, but before they become rubbery. Remove from the heat.

7   Divide the rice among four bowls. Cover one half of the rice in each bowl with the egg mixture and the other half with the mince mixture. Top with the spring onion and serve.

GYŪDON
SOY-SIMMERED BEEF

Gyūdon is Japan's fast food, a salty-sweet mix of piping-hot, finely sliced beef and onions simmered in soy, sake and mirin. The beef is ladled over a bowl of warm, fluffy rice, then topped with a Hot-spring egg (page 219) and sprinkled with Shichimi tōgarashi (page 227): a simple, fulfilling dish that has survived since 1899, when Eikichi Matsudah opened the first Yoshinoya restaurant in Nihonbashi, Tokyo.

SERVES 4

1 onion, finely sliced

1 × 3 cm (1¼ in) piece ginger, shredded

400 ml (13½ fl oz) Katsuo dashi (page 220)

125 ml (½ cup) light soy sauce

100 ml (3½ fl oz) sake

120 ml (4 fl oz) mirin

30 g (1 oz) caster (superfine) sugar

500 g (1 lb 2 oz) beef, finely sliced (see note)

rice, to serve

4 Hot-spring eggs (page 219), (optional)

Shichimi tōgarashi (page 227), to serve

beni shōga (pickled ginger), to serve

1   In a large saucepan, combine the onion, ginger, katsuo dashi, soy sauce, sake, mirin and sugar. Bring to a simmer over medium heat and cook for 5 minutes, then add the beef. Simmer for 10–15 minutes, regularly skimming away any impurities that rise to the surface, until the liquid has reduced by approximately one-quarter.

2   To serve, divide the rice between bowls. Spoon the beef over the rice and top with a hot-spring egg, if desired, shichimi tōgarashi and beni shōga.

Note
To easily slice beef very thinly, place it in the freezer for ½–1 hour, or until just firm but not frozen solid. Using a gentle back-and-forth motion, cut thin slices across the grain for the most tender results.
    Finely sliced beef can also be found in Asian, Japanese or Korean supermarkets in the freezer section.

KARĒ
JAPANESE CURRY

Watch any anime or visit any yōshoku (Western-style) restaurant and karē will inevitably show up. The intoxicating spice paste was first introduced to Japan in the 19th century by the British Empire and the officers of the Royal Navy, and has become so ingrained in Japanese culture it is considered a national dish.

Japan's first curry recipe appeared in a Japanese cookbook in 1872, with restaurants serving the dish in 1886. At that time, curry powder was a luxurious spice, imported from British firm Crosse & Blackwell, the world's first curry powder company. It wasn't until 1923 that Minejiro Yamasaki created a Japanese-made curry powder. This later became known as S&B Curry, one of Japan's foremost Japanese curry brands.

The early 1900s saw a flurry of curry inventions. Karē udon, noodles in a thick curry broth with a hint of soy, was created in Tokyo in 1904, while katsu karē, a crumbed pork cutlet with curry sauce, appeared in Tokyo in 1918. Karē pan, curry stuffed in a fried bun, was first invented in 1927, and can be found today in all of Japan's bakeries, including French outposts Paul Bocuse and Le Pain de Joël Robuchon.

But unlike its spicy origins, Japanese curry has a distinctive flavour of its own: a mellow warmth from the spices and a sweetness from apples, an essential ingredient grated into the roux-like mix (Vermont Curry – another popular Japanese brand –

includes honey). Potatoes and carrots are always added (and have been since 1910), along with a side of pickles to cut through the rich gravy.

So entrenched in Japanese culture is curry that it is served on Japan Maritime Self-Defense Force naval ships and canteens for lunch every Friday, a tradition stemming from the Imperial Japanese Navy (1868–1945). The Force's base in Yokosuka City in Kanagawa (south of Tokyo) is famous for its Yokosuka kaigun (navy) curry, said to be based on the original 1908 Imperial Japanese Navy recipe. Each May, a Yokosuka Curry Festival is held, with different curries – recipes from each JMSDF ship – featured alongside specialty curries from other Japanese regions.

Neighbourhoods in Japan hold annual curry festivals, dedicated to the glories of karē pan and curry. At Ikebukuro's former curry pan festival, over 150 bakeries gathered to showcase their baked or deep-fried creations, filled with prawns (shrimp), cheese, corn, hard-boiled eggs, A5 wagyu and Kobe beef. Shimokitazawa holds an annual curry festival and Kanda, a Curry Grand Prix.

KĪMAKARĒ

KEEMA CURRY

Curry, or karē, has a long history in Japan and is so beloved by the Japanese that it has been adopted as a national cuisine. Peruse the karē aisle of a Japanese supermarket and you'll find hundreds of varieties of instant curry roux and curries in retort pouches, which can be quickly warmed up in hot water or a microwave. Japan's astronauts even eat retort karē in space.

We are partial to the instant Japanese curries for a quick, delicious dinner, but this keema karē is – despite the long ingredient list – just as easy to make with more depth of flavour.

The left-over curry can also be kept aside and used as a filling for delicious Curry buns (page 127), another Japanese favourite.

SERVES 4

1 tomato

2 tablespoons neutral oil,
  for frying

400 g (14 oz) minced
  (ground) pork or chicken

1 onion, diced

1 carrot, diced

1 garlic clove, finely chopped

1 × 3 cm (1¼ in) piece ginger,
  peeled and finely chopped

1 tablespoon tomato paste
  (concentrated puree)

600 ml (20¼ fl oz) chicken
  stock or water

1 apple, peeled and grated

1 bay leaf

2 tablespoons akamiso
  (red miso paste)

1 tablespoon sesame oil

½ tablespoon honey

1 tablespoon soy sauce

rice, to serve

4 Hot-spring eggs (page 219),
  to serve

1 bunch spring onions
  (scallions), finely sliced

Spice mix (see note)

1 tablespoon cumin seeds

4 tablespoons Japanese
  curry powder

1 tablespoon ground coriander

1 tablespoon garam masala

1 tablespoon ground cumin

1 teaspoon ground cardamom

1 teaspoon ground cinnamon

Note
If you don't feel like making the
spice mix for this recipe, you can
substitute 1 block of curry roux in
its place.

1   Combine all of the spice mix ingredients in a bowl and
set aside.

2   Using a sharp knife, score a cross into the skin of the tomato.
Fill a large bowl with iced water. Bring a large saucepan of water
to the boil over high heat. Blanch the tomato in the boiling water
for 10 seconds, then transfer to the iced water using a slotted
spoon. Peel the tomato by pulling the skin away from the cross.
Chop the flesh of the tomato and set aside.

3   In a large saucepan, heat 1 tablespoon of the oil over medium-
high heat. Fry the mince until browned, breaking up any chunks
with the back of a wooden spoon, then remove from the pan and
set aside.

4   Return the pan to the heat. Add another tablespoon of the
oil and fry the onion, carrot, garlic and ginger until soft but not
coloured. Add the spice mix and fry until fragrant, then add the
tomato paste and cook, stirring constantly, until it darkens.

5   Add the stock, tomato, apple and mince and bring to the boil,
then add the bay leaf. Reduce the heat to low and simmer for
30 minutes, stirring occasionally so that the mixture doesn't stick
to the bottom of the pan.

6   When ready to serve, remove from the heat and stir through
the miso, sesame oil, honey and soy sauce. Divide the rice
between bowls and top each one with the curry, a hot-spring
egg and spring onions.

BĪFU SHICHŪ

BEEF STEW

This French-style beef stew draws inspiration from hayashi beef, a popular yōshoku (Western-style) dish in Japan. Hayashi beef was first created in the early 1900s, but the origin of its name remains unknown; stories suggest that it could be named after a chef called Hayashi, or be the Japanese–English interpretation of 'hashed beef'.

Back then, it was enjoyed over a bed of hot rice, and it still is today, though we've also included it as a filling for a grilled sandwich (see page 124).

SERVES 4, WITH EXTRA TO MAKE BEEF STEW JAFFLES (PAGE 124)

1 kg (2 lb 3 oz) stewing beef, cut into 4 pieces

2 tablespoons plain (all-purpose) flour

2 tablespoons neutral oil, for frying

1 garlic bulb, halved crossways

2 onions, roughly chopped

2 carrots, roughly chopped

2 celery stalks, peeled and roughly chopped

100 ml (3½ fl oz) brandy

100 ml (3½ fl oz) vermouth

400 ml (13½ fl oz) red wine

3 sprigs parsley

1 bay leaf

500 ml (2 cups) beef stock

2 tablespoons potato starch

2 tablespoons unsalted butter

rice, to serve

1   Preheat the oven to 150°C (300°F), unless you are using a slow cooker. Coat the beef in the flour.

2   In a saucepan or a flameproof casserole dish large enough to hold everything, heat the oil over high heat. Add the beef and brown on all sides, then remove and set aside. Reduce the heat to medium, add the garlic and fry until golden brown. Remove and set aside with the beef. Add the onion, carrot and celery to the pan and fry until coloured. Remove and set aside with the beef.

3   Deglaze the pan with the brandy and vermouth and simmer until the liquid is reduced by half.

4   If using a slow cooker, pour the liquid into the slow cooker. Otherwise, add the wine, beef, garlic, vegetables, parsley and bay leaf to the pan, along with enough beef stock to cover all of the ingredients. If they are not fully submerged in the liquid, top up with water until they are. Bring to a simmer, cover with a lid and place in the oven for 4 hours.

5   If using a slow cooker, place the wine, beef, garlic, vegetables, parsley, bay leaf and beef stock in the slow cooker instead of the pan, topping up with water if necessary, and cook for 4 hours. (If your slow cooker has more than one setting, cook the beef on high.)

6   After 4 hours, remove the stew from the oven or slow cooker and strain the broth into another saucepan, discarding the parsley and bay leaf. Cook the broth over high heat until it is reduced by half. Mix the potato starch with 2 tablespoons of water to make a smooth paste and add to the broth to thicken. Reduce the heat to low, add the butter and stir to combine. Season to taste with salt and pepper.

7   Return the beef and vegetables to the broth to warm through and serve with rice.

MISO NASU GURATAN

MISO EGGPLANT GRATIN

Eggplant (aubergine) and miso are a wonderful combination, the salty-sweetness of the miso complementing the juicy, delicate-tasting flesh. This recipe is Japanese-meets-French, with a miso bechamel sauce mixed with eggplant and other vegetables to create a gratin.

SERVES 4 AS A MAIN

2 eggplants (aubergines)

200 g (7 oz) assorted vegetables such as pumpkin (winter squash), broccoli, carrot, bell pepper (capsicum) and mushrooms

2 tablespoons olive oil

125 g (1 cup) grated cheese

Miso bechamel sauce

20 g (¾ oz) unsalted butter

20 g (¾ oz) plain (all-purpose) flour

2 tablespoons sake

150 ml (5 fl oz) milk

50 g (1¾ oz) shiromiso (white miso paste)

1   First, make the miso bechamel. Melt the butter in a saucepan over medium-low heat. Add the flour and cook, stirring constantly, until the colour just begins to change, then add the sake. Stir to combine, then add the milk in three batches, stirring well after each addition. Whisk in the miso until well incorporated, then remove from the heat. Season with salt and pepper and set aside.

2   Preheat the oven to 200°C (400°F). Fill a large saucepan with water, place a large bamboo steamer on top and bring to the boil over medium heat.

3   Cut the eggplants in half lengthways. Hollow out the eggplant halves by cutting a crosshatch pattern into the flesh and scooping it out, taking care not to cut right through the skin. Reserve the eggplant flesh and the hollowed-out eggplant skins and set aside while you prepare the other vegetables.

4   Cut the assorted vegetables into bite-sized pieces. If you are using eggplant, bell pepper and/or mushrooms, heat the olive oil in a large frying pan over medium-high heat and stir-fry the vegetables until tender. Meanwhile, if you are using pumpkin, broccoli and/or carrot, steam until a knife passes through them easily.

5   Scrunch some foil and place in a baking tray to hold the eggplant skins in place while cooking. Mix the vegetables with the miso bechamel and fill the eggplant skins. Cover with cheese and bake for 20–30 minutes, or until browned; you may need to place the gratin under the grill (broiler) and cook for a further 5 minutes to achieve the browned top.

OMURAISU
OMELETTE RICE

Omuraisu is a yōshoku (Western-style) creation invented at the turn of the 20th century by a Ginza restaurant called Renga-tei (est. 1895, it is still serving omuraisu today). The rice may be wrapped within the omelette or tucked underneath, but either way, there is always ketchup: the tartness cuts through the rich egginess of the dish, particularly if you opt for the demi-glace sauce. Kawaii ketchup drawings – as seen on omurice in maid cafes – are optional.

SERVES 1

neutral oil, for frying

¼ onion, diced

2 button mushrooms, sliced

1 tablespoon diced ham

185 g (1 cup) cooked rice

1 teaspoon soy sauce

1 tablespoon tomato ketchup

3 eggs, beaten

Beef demi-glace (page 222)
   or tomato ketchup, to serve

1   Heat 1 tablespoon of oil in a 20 cm (8 in) frying pan over high heat. Stir-fry the onion, mushroom and ham until the onion is translucent. Add the rice to the pan and fry until warmed through, then add the soy sauce and ketchup and stir to combine. Transfer to a plate and keep warm.

2   Heat a clean non-stick frying pan over medium–high heat and add enough oil to cover the bottom. Pour out the excess oil so that only a thin coating is left, then add the eggs to the pan. Mix with chopsticks or a spatula until they are partially set but still runny.

3   Transfer the eggs to a large bowl and whisk them to break up the curds. Clean the frying pan, heat it back up and coat again with oil. Pour out the excess oil and return the eggs to the pan, using the side of the pan to flip and shape them into an oval.

4   When just set, carefully place the omelette on top of the rice and serve with demi-glace or more ketchup on top.

MENTAIKO PASUTA

PASTA WITH SPICY POLLOCK ROE

Mentaiko pasta is said to have been invented in Tokyo in the 1960s by a tiny store selling wafu pasta – Italian pasta with Japanese toppings. It is a seemingly strange combination: spicy pollock roe with soy sauce, aonori (powdered seaweed flakes) and butter, but have a taste and you'll find that it's incredibly addictive.

The spicy, salty mentaiko gives the dish a wonderful depth and umami, in the same way that karasumi (bottarga) and caviar can change a simple pasta's flavour dramatically. The dish can get rather rich, so the sharp, citrusy tang of lemon and the distinctive herbal taste of shiso (perilla) leaf are essential to cut through the richness.

SERVES 2

180 g (6¼ oz) dried spaghetti

60 g (2 oz) mentaiko (spicy pollock roe), plus extra to serve

30 g (1 oz) unsalted butter, at room temperature

2 tablespoons soy sauce

50 ml (1¾ fl oz) cream (optional)

1 teaspoon freshly ground black pepper

1 bunch shiso (perilla) leaves, shredded

1 teaspoon aonori (powdered seaweed flakes; see glossary)

½ lemon, cut into wedges

1 tablespoon kizami nori (finely shredded nori; see glossary)

½ cucumber, julienned

1   Cook the pasta according to the instructions on the packet.

2   While the pasta is cooking, combine the mentaiko, butter, soy sauce, cream (if using) and pepper in a large bowl.

3   Reserve 250 ml (1 cup) of the pasta water before draining the spaghetti. Add the pasta to the mentaiko mixture and combine, adding enough of the reserved pasta water to create a velvety sauce. Divide between two bowls and top with the remaining ingredients.

UNI PASUTA

SEA URCHIN PASTA

Uni (sea urchin). It's an acquired taste for some, but for others, it's a little orange sliver of heaven. Uni season is eagerly anticipated in Japan, with the best uni coming from the chilly waters of Hokkaido. The prized ingredient is a luxury, the top grades served in sushi-ya (sushi restaurants) as is, or as uni gunkan (with sushi rice and a strip of nori). Then there's the incredibly luxurious uni and ikura don, a bowl of rice topped with glimmering salmon roe and lashings of sea urchin.

This decadent dish is a yōshoku (Western-style) creation: a combination of uni and salmon roe or caviar with pasta. It is creamy, sweet and salty, with a lovely burst of brininess from the caviar and sea urchin.

SERVES 4

400 g (14 oz) dried spaghetti

160 g (5¾ oz) uni (sea urchin), cleaned

125 ml (½ cup) dry white wine

250 ml (1 cup) cream

olive oil, to serve

4 teaspoons caviar or salmon roe

chopped chives, to serve

1   Cook the pasta according to the instructions on the packet. In the meantime, mash half of the uni to create a paste.

2   Bring the wine to the boil in a saucepan over medium heat and cook until reduced by half. Stir in the cream and allow to come to a simmer, then reduce the heat to low. Add the mashed uni and mix through. Season to taste with salt and pepper.

3   Reserve 250 ml (1 cup) of the pasta water before draining the spaghetti. Add the pasta to the uni mixture and combine, adding enough of the reserved pasta water to create a velvety sauce.

4   Divide between plates and dress with the remaining uni. Drizzle with olive oil and top each plate with a teaspoon of caviar and a sprinkle of chives. Serve on its own as a starter or with a side salad as a main.

BENTŌ

Bentō first emerged during the Azuchi–Momoyama period (1573–1603), when they were packed for nobility in beautifully lacquered wooden boxes for outdoor excursions such as hanami (cherry blossom viewing) and tea ceremonies.

In the Edo period (1603–1868), bentō flourished, with the makunochi bentō ('makunochi' meaning the interval between a play) coming into vogue. Patrons of Noh and Kabuki theatre would bring makunochi bentō filled with sesame-sprinkled onigiri (rice balls) and a variety of side dishes to enjoy during intermissions.

The Meiji Era (1868–1912) heralded the arrival of ekiben (train station bentō), a result of Japan's developing railway system. The first simple eki-ben comprised two onigiri with a serving of takuan (pickled daikon/Japanese radish), and was sold at Utsunomiya Station in Tochigi Prefecture in 1885.

Today, Japanese train stations brim with ekiben shops, which sell everything from humble onigiri and seasonal themed bentō, to bentō filled with prized beef, scallops, uni (sea urchin) and clams from renowned prefectures.

Bentō can also be found in konbini (convenience stores), depachika (department store food halls) and at famous restaurants, which create elaborate bentō for special occasions such as hanami, hinamatsuri (Girls' Day) and the Japanese New Year (when they are called osechi ryōri and are packed in special boxes called jūbako).

The following are a few bentō suggestions that offer a balanced meal of carbohydrates, protein and vegetables. If visiting Japan, we recommend (Tokyu) Hands and Loft for an incredible range of bentō accessories and bentō. Beautiful but expensive lacquered and magewappa (Akita cedar) bentō can be found in the kitchen sections of department stores.

Suggested bentō combinations

Soy-simmered beef (page 61)

+ Jako salad (page 88)
+ rice

Onigiri (page 78)

+ Marinated fried chicken (page 116)
+ Rolled egg omelette (page 32)
+ Japanese pickles (pages 18–25)

Mince stir-fry with potatoes (page 58)

+ Dashi-marinated greens with sesame sauce (page 80)
+ rice

Salt-grilled salmon (page 28)

+ umeboshi (pickled plum)
+ Dashi-simmered vegetables (page 110)
+ rice

Tofu patties (page 105)

+ Tomato salad with ume dressing (page 90)
+ Chilled eggplant with ponzu and shredded katsuobushi (page 82)
+ Soy-seasoned egg (page 150)

Chilled beef shabu salad (page 85)

+ Onigiri (page 78)
+ Mushrooms with sesame-tofu dressing (page 84)
+ Miso-grilled tofu (page 83)

Broad bean rice (page 111)

+ Fried chicken with tartare sauce (page 117)
+ Sauteed root vegetables (page 79)

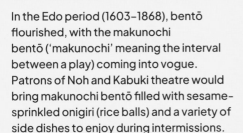

←

From left: Marinated fried chicken (page 116), Onigiri (page 78) with salted seaweed (back) and salted salmon (front), Jako salad (page 88).

ONIGIRI
RICE BALLS

Onigiri has a long history in Japan, dating back to 300 BCE, when it took the form of chimaki, or glutinous rice wrapped in bamboo leaves. In the 11th century, the humble rice ball was mentioned in the writings of Lady Murasaki (973–1020), and samurai were known to have eaten onigiri on the battlefield in the 17th century. It wasn't until the Edo period (1603–1868) that the glutinous rice and bamboo leaves were replaced with Japanese rice and nori.

Today, onigiri is sold in train stations and konbini (convenience stores). Most kaiseki restaurants also offer to turn the remaining rice from the rice course into onigiri for guests to enjoy the next day. Onigiri is called nigirimeshi or omusubi in some regions, omusubi being the triangular- or mountain-shaped variety.

Onigiri takes two forms: plain rice with a filling, and flavoured rice cooked with ingredients such as Konbu dashi (page 221), mirin and soy sauce. Grains such as barley and buckwheat can also be added.

Our favourite onigiri variations are shio konbu (dried salted kelp) mixed through plain rice, and yaki onigiri: rice brushed with soy sauce then grilled.

1 teaspoon salt
warm cooked rice
fillings (see below)
nori (optional)

Filling ideas

umeboshi (pickled plum)
Salt-grilled salmon (page 28), flaked
Soy-seasoned egg (page 150)
mentaiko (spicy pollock roe)
tinned tuna mixed with mayonnaise
sauteed mushrooms
Braised pork (page 150)
Soy-simmered beef (page 61)

1   Fill a bowl with 1 cup of water, add the salt and wet your hands to prevent the rice from sticking to them. Take a handful of rice in one hand and place the filling in the centre.

2   Gently press the rice around the filling to form a ball or triangle shape. Wrap in nori, if desired, then serve.

KINPIRA
SAUTEED ROOT VEGETABLES

Kinpira is the Japanese method for lightly sauteing root vegetables (typically carrot, gobō – burdock root – and lotus root), leaving them crunchy and crisp. This recipe, which veers a little from tradition, is addictively salty and spicy, with heat from the chilli and chilli threads. It makes for a great beer snack.

SERVES 4 AS A SIDE

1 tablespoon sesame seeds

2 tablespoons sesame oil

300 g (10½ oz) firm root vegetables such as carrot, kohlrabi, gobō (burdock root) and lotus root, peeled and cut into matchsticks

1 tablespoon soy sauce

1 dried red chilli

1 tablespoon dried chilli threads

1   In a small frying pan over medium heat, dry-fry the sesame seeds until golden brown and fragrant. Transfer to a bowl and set aside.

2   Heat the sesame oil in a large frying pan over medium–high heat and stir-fry the vegetables until softened but retaining a little crunch. Add the toasted sesame seeds, soy sauce, dried chilli and chilli threads and stir to combine. Taste and season with salt if required.

3   Serve hot or cold; the kinpira will keep in the fridge for 3 days.

GOMA-AE

DASHI-MARINATED GREENS WITH SESAME SAUCE

A traditional Japanese meal would not be complete without an array of kobachi, or little side dishes, usually featuring seasonal vegetables. This dish of leafy greens blanched, briefly marinated and dressed with a nutty sesame sauce is a classic.

SERVES 4 AS A SIDE

1 bunch leafy greens such as watercress, spinach or snow pea (mangetout) tendrils

250 ml (1 cup) Katsuo dashi or Konbu dashi (pages 220–221), chilled

1½ teaspoons mirin

1½ teaspoons light soy sauce

½ teaspoon salt

Goma-ae (sesame sauce)

2 tablespoons sesame seeds, plus extra to finish

1 teaspoon caster (superfine) sugar

1 tablespoon soy sauce

1 teaspoon sake

2 tablespoons Konbu dashi (page 221)

1   Fill a large bowl with iced water. Bring a large saucepan of water to the boil over high heat and blanch the greens in the boiling water very briefly, until just wilted. Using tongs or a slotted spoon, transfer the greens to the iced water to refresh. Squeeze dry and set aside.

2   Combine the dashi, mirin, light soy sauce and salt in a container. Immerse the greens in the liquid and leave for 15 minutes to marinate.

3   Meanwhile, with a mortar and pestle or suribachi (traditional Japanese grinder), grind the sesame seeds and sugar into a thick paste. Incorporate the remaining ingredients to create a sauce with the consistency of thick cream, adding a little more dashi if the mixture is too thick.

4   Transfer the greens to a serving bowl and arrange into a neat pile. Pour the marinade over the greens and spoon over the sesame sauce. Sprinkle with some extra sesame seeds to finish.

→

A selection of classic side dishes. Clockwise from top left: Sauteed root vegetables (page 79), Chilled eggplant with ponzu and shredded katsuobushi (page 82), Mushrooms with sesame-tofu dressing (page 84), Miso-grilled tofu (page 83), Potato salad (page 89), Dashi-marinated greens with sesame sauce.

HISUI NASU

CHILLED EGGPLANT WITH PONZU AND SHREDDED KATSUOBUSHI

In this simple, elegant side dish, eggplants are deep-fried and peeled to reveal the pale green flesh beneath – hence 'hisui', which means jade in Japanese.

SERVES 4 AS A SIDE

3 Japanese, Lebanese or other long, slender eggplants (aubergines)

neutral oil, for deep-frying

60 ml (¼ cup) Ponzu (page 225)

1 handful of katsuobushi (dried skipjack tuna flakes), finely shredded

1   Fill a large bowl with iced water and set aside. Cut the tops and bottoms off the eggplants and make four shallow cuts running down the length of each one.

2   Fill a large, heavy-based saucepan one-third of the way with oil. Heat over medium heat until small bubbles form on the surface of a wooden chopstick inserted into the oil – approximately 160°C (320°F).

3   Deep-fry the eggplant for 3–5 minutes, or until tender – a knife inserted near the top of the eggplant should easily slip through – and transfer to the iced water using a slotted spoon.

4   When the eggplants are cool enough to handle, peel and discard the skin. Dry the eggplant flesh thoroughly with paper towels and cut into bite-sized pieces. Dress with the ponzu and top with the shredded katsuobushi.

TOFU DENGAKU

MISO-GRILLED TOFU

Traditionally slathered with different types of miso, then skewered and grilled over hot coals, tofu dengaku dates back to 1437, when it was one of the most popular recipes of the Muromachi period (1338–1600). The clean, pure taste of the tofu highlights the salty-sweetness of the miso, bringing out the best flavours of both ingredients.

SERVES 4 AS A SIDE

- 1 × 500 g (1 lb 2 oz) block momen (firm) tofu
- 50 g (1¾ oz) hatchōmiso (see glossary)
- 250 g (9 oz) shiromiso (white miso paste)
- 100 ml (3½ fl oz) sake
- 2 tablespoons caster (superfine) sugar
- 1 tablespoon neutral oil, for frying

1   The day before you plan to make tofu dengaku, prepare the tofu to remove excess moisture and improve its texture and flavour.

2   Line a plate with paper towels. Bring a saucepan of water to the boil over high heat, add the tofu and boil for 5 minutes. Drain the tofu and transfer to the lined plate. Cover the tofu with another layer of paper towels and place a second plate on top, then weigh the plate down with something heavy, like tinned goods or a wooden chopping board. Transfer to the fridge and leave overnight.

3   The next day, cut the tofu into 10 cm × 4 cm (4 in × 1½ in) pieces. Soak bamboo skewers in water for 15–20 minutes to prevent them from burning while cooking. Thread each tofu piece onto a skewer and set aside.

4   To make the miso sauce, place the remaining ingredients, except the oil, in a saucepan over medium heat and cook, stirring constantly, until the sugar dissolves. Remove from the heat and set aside to cool.

5   Preheat the grill (broiler) to medium. Heat the oil in a non-stick frying pan over medium heat and fry the tofu pieces until golden brown on both sides. Transfer the tofu to a baking tray, spread each piece with a teaspoon of miso sauce, and grill (broil) until the miso is bubbling and browned. Serve immediately or at room temperature.

KINOKO NO SHIRA-AE

MUSHROOMS WITH SESAME-TOFU DRESSING

Shira-ae – sesame seeds mixed with tofu to make a dressing – is an elevated form of goma-ae (sesame sauce; see page 80), but we find it hard to pick a favourite between the two! The tofu adds a wonderful creaminess to the dressing: a perfect match with leafy greens.

SERVES 4 AS A SIDE

1 tablespoon sesame seeds

125 g (4½ oz) momen (firm) tofu

500 ml (2 cups) Konbu dashi
(page 221)

1 tablespoon salt, plus extra
to taste

1 bunch enoki mushrooms,
cut into 2 cm (¾ in) lengths

150 g (5½ oz) shiitake
mushrooms, finely sliced

150 g (5½ oz) oyster mushrooms,
torn

100 g (3½ oz) spinach or other
leafy green vegetable

1   Using a mortar and pestle or suribachi (traditional Japanese grinder), grind the sesame seeds into a coarse powder. Add the tofu and 1 tablespoon of the konbu dashi and grind until the mixture is the consistency of thick cream, adding a little more dashi if it is too thick. Taste and season with a little salt if required.

2   Fill a large bowl with iced water. Heat the remaining dashi and 1 tablespoon of salt in a large saucepan over medium heat. Simmer the mushrooms in the dashi until softened, approximately 5 minutes.

3   Using a slotted spoon, transfer the mushrooms to a colander and leave to drain. Increase the heat to high and bring the dashi to the boil. Add the spinach and cook until just wilted, then drain and transfer to the bowl of iced water. Once cool, drain again and squeeze dry.

4   Combine the mushrooms and spinach in a serving bowl, coat with the tofu mix and serve.

HIYASHI GYŪ SHABU

CHILLED BEEF SHABU SALAD

This refreshing salad, perfect for the hot Japanese summers, is a twist on the traditional shabu–shabu, where pork or beef is cooked with a quick swish in hot broth (see page 191). We've used Japanese vegetables and herbs such as shiso (perilla) leaf and mizuna (Japanese mustard greens), which can be found in Asian greengrocers. Shiso has a distinct flavour and is hard to replace, but mizuna can be substituted with other greens like rocket (arugula) or spinach.

SERVES 4 AS A STARTER

200 g (7 oz) finely sliced beef (see note)

1 handful of mizuna (Japanese mustard greens)

1 Lebanese (short) cucumber, seeds removed, julienned

½ leek, white part only, julienned

1 carrot, julienned

½ bunch shiso (perilla) leaves, julienned

Dressing

2 tablespoons sesame seeds

2 tablespoons soy sauce

2 tablespoons Katsuo dashi (page 220) or water

1 tablespoon mirin

1 onion, grated

1 tablespoon grated ginger

1 tablespoon oil

1   First, make the dressing. In a small frying pan over medium heat, dry-fry the sesame seeds until golden brown and fragrant. Transfer to a bowl, add the remaining dressing ingredients and stir to combine, then set aside.

2   Fill a large bowl with iced water. Bring a large saucepan of water to a simmer over medium heat and blanch the beef in the water briefly until it just changes colour, then immediately transfer it to the iced water to stop the cooking process. Drain well.

3   On a serving plate, layer the mizuna on the bottom, then the beef, followed by the julienned vegetables. Pour the dressing over to finish.

Note
Finely sliced beef can also be found in Asian, Japanese or Korean supermarkets in the freezer section.

JAKO
SARADA

JAKO SALAD

This is one of our favourite salads: a refreshing combination of chilled silken tofu blocks, crisp leaves and crunchy jako (dried baby sardines). Brilliant in summer, it keeps well in lunch bentō.

SERVES 4 AS A SIDE

1 tablespoon sesame seeds

30 g (1 oz) jako (dried baby sardines; see glossary) or other dried small white fish

2 tablespoons soy sauce

2 tablespoons rice vinegar

1 tablespoon sesame oil

½ daikon (Japanese radish), julienned

1 bunch mizuna (Japanese mustard greens)

2 tablespoons chopped chives

1 shallot, finely sliced

1 × 200 g (7 oz) block silken tofu, cut into 8 cubes

1   In a small frying pan over medium heat, dry-fry the sesame seeds until golden brown and fragrant. Transfer to a bowl and set aside.

2   Place the jako in the hot frying pan and dry-fry over medium heat until crispy. Transfer to a separate bowl and set aside.

3   Add the soy sauce, rice vinegar and sesame oil to the toasted sesame seeds and mix well to make a dressing.

4   Combine the vegetables and herbs in a large mixing bowl and dress with the sesame-soy dressing. Place the tofu in the centre of a serving dish, arrange the salad around it, and top with the jako.

POTATO SARADA

POTATO SALAD

Every Japanese izakaya has a signature potato salad recipe, and our restaurant, chotto, was no exception. The potato salad was one of our most popular kobachi (side dishes), and while this version is simplified, it is still delicious. We like leaving the potatoes chunky, breaking them up just enough for the dressing to make its way into the crevices. For a quintessentially Japanese flavour, we recommend using Kewpie mayonnaise.

SERVES 4 AS A SIDE

500 g (1 lb 2 oz) potatoes, skin on

1 tablespoon salt, plus extra to taste

1 teaspoon dijon mustard

1 teaspoon rice vinegar

1 teaspoon neri goma (Japanese sesame paste; see glossary)

1 teaspoon soy sauce

1 tablespoon neutral oil

50 g (1¾ oz) bacon (optional)

2 tablespoons mayonnaise (homemade or Kewpie)

1 shallot, finely sliced

50 g (1¾ oz) mixed pickled vegetables such as cucumber, fennel and carrot, chopped

1 hard-boiled egg, chopped

1   Fill a large saucepan with water and add the potatoes and salt. Bring to the boil and cook until a knife easily passes through the middle of a potato, then drain in a colander and leave to cool and dry for 10 minutes. Peel the potatoes and transfer to a large mixing bowl. Add the mustard, rice vinegar, neri goma, soy sauce and oil and stir well to combine (it is fine if the potatoes break up slightly). Set aside to cool.

2   In a frying pan over medium heat, fry the bacon until crispy (if using), then drain and break up into small pieces.

3   Spread the mayonnaise on the bottom of a serving bowl. Add the potatoes, then the shallot, followed by the pickles. Scatter the egg and bacon over the top, season with salt and pepper, and serve. Mix together at the table, breaking the potatoes into bite-sized pieces. Leftovers can be kept in the fridge for 1 day, and make a great addition to bentō.

TOMATO SALAD WITH UME DRESSING

This modern salad combines luscious, sweet tomatoes with a delicious Japanese dressing of tofu, umeboshi (pickled plum) and ume vinegar. It's best eaten in summer when tomatoes are at their peak; we also recommend using heirloom varieties. The ume vinegar and umeboshi are essential for the tartness they bring; the bacon, which adds a wonderful crunch, is entirely optional.

SERVES 4 AS A SIDE

2 slices bacon (optional)

3 tomatoes

200 g (7 oz) assorted sprouts such as mung bean, snow pea (mangetout) and alfalfa

1 tablespoon shredded shiso (perilla) leaves

1 shallot, finely sliced

1 umeboshi (pickled plum), seed removed, torn into small pieces

Dressing

100 g (3½ oz) silken tofu

2 tablespoons ume vinegar (or 1 umeboshi and 1 tablespoon rice vinegar)

1 teaspoon caster (superfine) sugar

1 tablespoon neutral oil

1   In a frying pan over medium heat, fry the bacon until crispy (if using), then drain and break up into small pieces.

2   To make the dressing, blend or mix the silken tofu, ume vinegar, sugar and oil together until homogenous. Season with salt and pepper to taste.

3   Cut the tomatoes into bite-sized pieces and place in a mixing bowl. Combine with the sprouts, shiso and shallot, then transfer to a serving bowl and top with the dressing, bacon and umeboshi.

MEN

The Japanese word for noodles

The sound of slurping hits us as we take our seats. It's easy to presume that it's the guys. After all, isn't slurping a man thing? But then, an immaculate Japanese woman in her twenties takes a seat beside us, graceful and demure. The ramen chef prepares her bowl with swift, precise movements, placing it on the counter in front of her. She takes a gentle sip of the broth first, then picks up her chopsticks, gathers some ramen and … slurps. Loudly, noisily.

Entering a noodle shop – any noodle shop – in Japan is always a culture shock for the uninitiated. The sound of slurping is overwhelming. (Also overwhelming is the ability of slender Japanese women to down not just a bowl of ramen, but an entire set, including fried rice, sometimes gyoza and a pint of beer.)

But it's a necessary thing. Ramen and udon in Japan are served in incredibly hot broths (especially tsukemen – you know you've stuffed up when your broth grows cold before you finish the noodles). Slurping helps cool down the noodles, and draws air in which intensifies the flavour of the soup.

Noodles first appeared in ancient Japan in the Heian period (794–1185). Brought over by Zen Buddhist monks from China's Song dynasty, soba, udon and sōmen would gradually spread throughout Japan, becoming popular during the Edo years (1603–1868). In particular, soba yatai (food carts) flourished in Edo (modern-day Tokyo), with one of the most popular yatai, Kendon Sobaya, enshrined in the artist Utagawa Toyokuni's ukiyo-e (woodblock) prints.

Ramen was a much later migrant, arriving in Japan's port city of Yokohama in the late 19th century. Named after China's lā mièn (hand-pulled noodles), it inspired a new wave of Tokyo yatai that started selling the noodle soup in the old neighbourhoods of Ueno and Asakusa in the early 20th century. While ramen in Japan today has its own distinctive styles, broths and toppings, shops selling chūka soba (meaning 'Chinese soba' – not to be confused with the Japanese buckwheat soba noodles) most closely reflect its origins, with a light shōyu (soy sauce) broth, chāshū (roast pork), spring onions (scallions) and wontons.

The different styles of men

Soba

Made from buckwheat, soba is most closely associated with Tokyo, though regional variations can be found all over Japan. In its simplest form (zaru soba; page 96), the noodles are quickly cooked, chilled and served on a slatted bamboo tray with nothing but wasabi, spring onions and tsuyu (soba dipping sauce) as accompaniments. Soba-yu, the water in which the soba is cooked, is usually requested at the end to pour into the tsuyu, creating a delicious broth. During the hot, sticky Japanese summers, however, this is an entirely optional step.

In winter, soba is cooked in hot broths, with toppings including kamo nanban (duck meat and spring onion), tororo (sticky grated yam), nameko mushrooms, sansai (mountain vegetables), tempura, kitsune (deep-fried tofu) and tsukimi (raw egg).

Fun fact #1: Tsukimi means moon viewing, with the moon represented by the raw egg. Kitsune, on the other hand, means fox. The same style of soba is known in the Kantō region as Tanuki (racoon dog).

Fun fact #2: On New Year's Eve, it's tradition to eat toshikoshi soba (long soba noodles). Toshikoshi means 'year crossing', signifying the end of the old year, the letting go of its regrets, and the beginning of the new one. This tradition originated in Edo times and is the busiest day for soba shops.

Udon

Udon, which is made from wheat flour, salt and water, also took flight in the Edo period, though it is perhaps more popular in Japan's south than in Tokyo. The most popular style is sanuki, a thick and flat variety from Kagawa, home of udon. Like soba, it can be eaten zaru-style; another chilled variety is bukkake udon, which features a thick dashi broth. As with soba, udon can be topped with a variety of ingredients, from spring onions, deep-fried tofu, wakame seaweed and tempura to more modern incarnations such as curry, mochi, meat and raw egg.

Fun fact #1: Udon topped with mochi is called chikara udon, meaning 'power udon'. Udon topped with meat and raw egg is called sutamina udon – 'stamina udon'.

Sōmen

Sōmen is also made from wheat, but unlike its plumper cousin, udon, it is delicate, white and slender. The noodle, which hails from Hyōgo Prefecture, was once served as an Imperial Court dish during the Tanabata Festival (7 July), but is now considered a noodle of summer, served over ice with ingredients such as cucumber and crab. Perhaps the most fun way to eat sōmen is nagashi-style, where the noodles are cast into a bamboo slide filled with ice-cold running water. Diners sit on either side of the slide, catching the sōmen with chopsticks as it drifts by.

Ramen

Ramen is a combination of wheat flour, salt and kansui, an alkaline liquid that turns the noodle yellow and gives it a springy texture. Like udon, it comes in a variety of styles, from straight to curly, soft to firm, narrow to wide and flat to thick. Ramen became incredibly trendy in the eighties, when specialty shops, each with their signature ramen style, started to emerge. While regional varieties such as Hakata's incredibly pungent tonkotsu (pork bone broth) ramen, Hokkaido's miso ramen and Tokyo's shio (salt) and shōyu ramen continue to be classics, the new band of chefs are pushing the envelope, scorching ramen broth in 300°C (570°F) lard in a fiery display (the signature of Gogyo Ramen in Kyoto) or adding clams, dried squid and sake lees, among other adventurous toppings.

Yokohama – ramen's birthplace – is the best place to try the dish (we also recommend Tokyo Station's Ramen Street, which features a rotating series of restaurants from Tokyo and all over the country). The picturesque port town is home to the Shin-Yokohama Ramen Museum, a ramen 'theme park' featuring nine subterranean ramen shops in a setting reminiscent of Japan in 1958.

Eat your fill (they do have mini bowls, so it is possible to squeeze more than one in) before heading to a museum of another sort: Momofuku Ando's Cup Noodles Museum, an incredibly well-thought-out exhibition space and factory exploring the birth of Chicken Ramen, the world's first instant noodles. Design your own Cup Noodles (a Japanese classic), then knock yourself out in the gift shop with kawaii items featuring Nissin's unbelievably cute mascot, Hiyoko-chan, and inspirational t-shirts bearing Momofuku Ando's philosophy.

✳ ZARU SOBA

Soba is one of those wonderfully versatile noodles that can be enjoyed in all of Japan's seasons. In summer, the chilled strands and dipping sauce are a welcome respite from the heat, and in spring and autumn, we like adding soba-yu (the starchy water the noodles are boiled in) to the soba tsuyu (dipping sauce) to form a warm, salty broth spiked with a little wasabi. In winter, soba is best enjoyed in a rich soup, the most popular being kamo nanban soba, with duck breast and negi (spring onion/scallion). We've also had soba in Matsumoto, simply served in a hot broth with a side of delicious, crisp tempura matsutake mushrooms – a real treat.

The art of making soba noodles is difficult and requires many years of practice. We've given a simple recipe for soba noodles here, though good dry soba noodles can be found in many Asian and Japanese supermarkets. This recipe is for zaru soba, which is a simple, chilled soba dish. You may choose to tempura some mushrooms, sweet potato or seafood to accompany it.

SERVES 2

½ bunch spring onions (scallions), finely sliced

½ daikon (Japanese radish), grated

wasabi, to serve

Soba noodles

400 g (14 oz) buckwheat flour

100 g (⅔ cup) plain (all-purpose) flour

potato starch, to dust

Soba tsuyu (soba dipping sauce)

300 ml (10¼ fl oz) Katsuo dashi or Konbu dashi (pages 220–221)

1 tablespoon caster (superfine) sugar

75 ml (2½ fl oz) soy sauce

75 ml (2½ fl oz) mirin

1   To make the soba noodles, combine the flours in a large bowl and stir in 150 ml (5 fl oz) of water. Once incorporated, add another 50 ml (1¾ fl oz) of water, mixing thoroughly before adding a final 50 ml (1¾ fl oz) of water. Roll the dough into a smooth ball, adding a little more water if the dough is too stiff.

2   Press the dough into a large oval, then roll out into a large rectangle about 3 mm (⅛ in) thick. Dust the dough with potato starch and fold into thirds, as though you were folding a letter for mailing. Dust again with potato starch and use a sharp knife to cut into noodles 3 mm (⅛ in) wide.

3   To make the soba tsuyu, combine the dashi and sugar in a small saucepan over low heat, cooking just long enough for the sugar to dissolve. Remove from the heat and allow to cool, then add the soy sauce and mirin.

4   Fill a large bowl with iced water and bring a large saucepan of water to the boil over high heat. Measure out 200 g (7 oz) soba noodles and cook in the boiling water for 1–2 minutes (or follow the packet instructions if you are using store-bought noodles). Drain the noodles and immediately transfer to the iced water to refresh. When the noodles are completely chilled, drain well.

5   Divide the noodles between two plates and the tsuyu between two small bowls. Serve the noodles with the bowls of tsuyu for dipping, accompanied by the spring onion, daikon and wasabi on the side.

YAKISOBA
FRIED NOODLES

Yakisoba first appeared in food stalls in Japan in the early 20th century, and is now a common fixture at matsuri (festivals). It's a simple, nostalgic dish: cabbage, carrot and pork belly sizzled over a hot plate, to which the noodles are added, then finished with a touch of yakisoba sauce, mayonnaise and a dusting of aonori (powdered seaweed flakes).

SERVES 4

500 g (1 lb 2 oz) fresh Ramen noodles (page 151)

1 tablespoon neutral oil, for frying

100 g (3½ oz) pork belly, finely sliced

1 onion, finely sliced

1 carrot, julienned

¼ cabbage, cut into square pieces

mayonnaise (preferably Kewpie), to serve

aonori (powdered seaweed flakes; see glossary), to serve

Yakisoba sauce

2 tablespoons oyster sauce

3 tablespoons tomato ketchup

1 tablespoon akamiso (red miso paste)

1 teaspoon caster (superfine) sugar

1 tablespoon soy sauce

1 tablespoon sake

freshly ground black pepper, to taste

1   First, make the yakisoba sauce. Combine all of the ingredients in a saucepan over low heat and cook just long enough to dissolve the sugar. Set aside to cool.

2   Bring a large saucepan of water to the boil over high heat and cook the noodles in the boiling water for 1–2 minutes (or follow the packet instructions if you are using store-bought noodles). Drain the noodles well.

3   Meanwhile, heat the oil in a large frying pan over high heat. Fry the pork until coloured, then add the onion and carrot and cook until softened. Add the cabbage, followed by the noodles. Fry until the cabbage begins to soften (it should still retain some crunch), then add 100 ml (3½ fl oz) of the yakisoba sauce to the pan. Toss the noodles to distribute the sauce evenly.

4   To serve, divide the noodles among four plates and top each one with a drizzle of mayonnaise and a sprinkling of aonori. Serve piping hot.

Note
Any left-over yakisoba sauce can be kept in the fridge for up to 1 month.

SUDACHI SŌMEN

Sudachi sōmen is a traditional Japanese summer dish: a salty, citrusy combination that also looks incredibly pretty. Thin slices of sudachi, a citrus fruit native to Tokushima, are placed on top of fine strands of sōmen and topped with grated daikon (Japanese radish), the combination of green and white evoking cool feelings. Sudachi is hard to find outside Japan, but can be substituted with lime. Sudachi sōmen is traditionally served as is, but we like adding crab.

SERVES 1

1 sudachi citrus or lime, skin on, scrubbed

1 bundle dried sōmen noodles

250 ml (1 cup) Katsuo dashi (page 220), chilled

1 tablespoon light soy sauce

1 teaspoon mirin

1 green chilli, seeded and finely sliced (optional)

50 g (1¾ oz) crabmeat (optional)

½ daikon (Japanese radish), grated

1   Using a mandoline or a sharp knife, thinly slice the citrus and set aside.

2   Fill a large bowl with iced water and bring a large saucepan of water to the boil over high heat. Cook the somen in the boiling water according to the packet instructions. Drain the noodles and immediately transfer to the iced water to refresh. When the noodles are completely chilled, drain well.

3   Combine the katsuo dashi, soy sauce and mirin in a bowl. Add the chilled sōmen and top with the citrus slices, chilli and crabmeat (if using), and a mound of grated daikon.

SHŌJIN RYŌRI
ZEN VEGETARIAN CUISINE

It is autumn in Japan. The rain is softly pattering on the changing colours of the maple trees outside. It's a mesmerising scene, enhanced by the austere setting of the dining room we are in: a large hall with nothing but tatami mats. There are no chairs and no tables. Instead, we kneel on two ribbons of red felt that run the length of the dining room.

A waitress brings out two trays, which she places on the floor. There's a square of goma dōfu (sesame tofu) with soy sauce and a dab of wasabi on top; a nimono (simmered) dish of shiitake mushroom, two snow peas (mangetout), a roll of yuba (bean curd skin) and fu (gluten); a selection of pickles and konnyaku (konjac gel); a hiryōzu (tofu patty) in gin-an sauce; rice and a thick miso soup; and a slice of kaki (persimmon) and two grapes to finish. The bowls are simple. There is nothing ostentatious. We are in Shigetsu, on the temple grounds of Tenryū-ji in Arashiyama, and this is shōjin ryōri.

Shōjin ryōri, or Zen vegetarian cuisine, was brought to Japan from China in the 13th century by the founder of Zen Buddhism – a monk named Dōgen. In accordance with Buddhist philosophy, only plant- and soy-based foods are used as ingredients, yet the dishes are elegant and satisfying. The 'rule of five' is used by the monks preparing the cuisine, with five colours (green, yellow, red, black and white) featuring in every meal, alongside the five flavours: sweet, sour, salty, bitter and umami. Shōjin ryōri's strong emphasis on seasonality would go on to influence kaiseki, Japan's haute cuisine of today.

A typical shōjin ryōri meal is composed of ichi-ju-san-sai: one soup and three dishes. The selection in the coming pages includes seven recipes, which can be prepared together to create an elaborate shōjin ryōri set, or cooked individually and served as a standalone vegetarian meal.

→
Clockwise from top left:
Sweetcorn soup (page 111), Broad bean rice (page 111),
Sesame tofu (page 104), Tofu patties (page 105),
Miso-grilled eggplant (page 106), Dashi-simmered
vegetables (page 110) and Tempura asparagus (page 107).

GOMA DŌFU
SESAME TOFU

Goma dōfu is one of the mainstays of shōjin ryōri. Despite its name, it doesn't contain any tofu or soy milk. It does, however, have a lovely, slightly firm texture and a nuttiness from the sesame paste.

MAKES 36 SMALL PIECES

100 g (3½ oz) neri goma
   (Japanese sesame paste;
   see glossary)

600 ml (20¼ fl oz) Konbu dashi
   (page 221)

100 ml (3½ fl oz) sake

60 g (2 oz) kuzu (arrowroot)
   starch

1 teaspoon salt

soy sauce, to serve

wasabi, to serve

1   Fill a 21 cm (8¼ in) square baking tin with cold water to a depth of 1 cm (½ in). If you don't have a baking tin with those exact dimensions, you can also use a smaller or larger tin; the tofu will end up thicker or thinner respectively.

2   Combine all of the ingredients, except the soy sauce and wasabi, in a large saucepan and whisk well to dissolve the kuzu starch. Place the saucepan over medium heat and begin to cook, stirring constantly and taking care to get into the sides. Make sure to keep stirring, or you will end up with lumpy tofu!

3   Cook for 10–15 minutes, or until the aroma of alcohol has dissipated and the mixture has thickened. Pour the water out of the baking tin and fill with the tofu mixture. Cover with heat-resistant plastic wrap and press the tofu into the corners of the tin, flattening out the top. Transfer to the fridge and chill for 3 hours or overnight, then cut into 3.5 cm (1½ in) cubes. The tofu will keep in the fridge for up to 3 days (see note).

4   To serve, divide the tofu between four bowls and top with soy sauce and a little dab of wasabi.

Note
The longer it rests, the firmer the tofu will become. By day three, it may be quite firm. If so, coat lightly in potato starch and deep-fry at 180°C (350°F). Serve with Gin-an sauce (page 223) for a delicious agedashi tōfu.

HIRYŌZU
TOFU PATTIES

Another common feature of shōjin ryōri, hiryōzu is a delicious patty made of tofu mixed with carrot, shiitake mushrooms, cloud ear fungus and lotus root, fried and served with an umami-rich Gin-an sauce (page 223). Hiryōzu keeps well in bentō, and we also love it with a dash of grated ginger on top.

**SERVES 4 AS PART OF
A SHŌJIN RYŌRI SET**

500 g (1 lb 2 oz) momen (firm) tofu

1 tablespoon oil

½ carrot, diced

3 fresh shiitake mushrooms, diced, or 3 dried shiitake mushrooms, rehydrated and diced

1 handful of fresh cloud ear fungus, diced, or 1 handful of dried wood ear fungus, rehydrated and diced

½ lotus root, diced

1 tablespoon soy sauce

1 tablespoon mirin

1 tablespoon sake

potato starch, to coat

neutral oil, for deep-frying

Gin-an sauce (page 223), to serve

1   The day before you plan to make hiryōzu, prepare the tofu to remove excess moisture and improve its texture and flavour.

2   Line a baking tray with paper towels. Bring a large saucepan of water to the boil over high heat, add the tofu and boil for 5 minutes. Drain the tofu and transfer to the lined tray. Cover the tofu with another layer of paper towels and place a second baking tray on top, then weigh the tray down with something heavy, like tinned goods or a wooden chopping board. Transfer to the fridge and leave overnight.

3   The next day, heat the oil in a large frying pan over medium-high heat and fry the carrot, shiitake mushroom, wood ear fungus and lotus root until softened but still retaining a little crunch. Add the soy sauce, mirin and sake and stir to combine. Season with salt to taste, then remove from the heat and allow to cool.

4   Remove the tofu from the fridge, place in the bowl of a food processor and blend until smooth. Transfer the tofu puree to a large mixing bowl and mix in the cooled vegetables. If the mixture is very soft, add potato starch until you have a dough-like consistency.

5   Fill a large, heavy-based saucepan one-third of the way with oil. Heat over medium heat to 180°C (350°F); a pinch of flour dropped into the oil should sizzle on contact.

6   Shape the tofu mixture into four patties, coat in potato starch and deep-fry until golden brown. Drain on paper towels and serve coated with gin-an sauce. Once fried, the patties can be cooled and frozen; they can be reheated by deep-frying again for 5 minutes or baking in the oven at 180°C (350°F) for 12–15 minutes.

NASU DENGAKU

MISO-GRILLED EGGPLANT

This dish is commonly seen in shōjin ryōri meals when eggplants (aubergines) are in season.

The combination of juicy, delicately sweet grilled (broiled) eggplant and salty miso is loved by both vegetarians and non-vegetarians, and can be found in izakaya throughout Japan in summer, when eggplants flourish.

SERVES 4 AS PART OF A SHŌJIN RYŌRI SET

1 eggplant (aubergine)
1 tablespoon neutral oil

Miso sauce

150 g (5½ oz) shiromiso (white miso paste)
50 g (1¾ oz) saikyo miso (see glossary)
50 ml (1¾ fl oz) sake
50 ml (1¾ fl oz) mirin
50 g (1¾ oz) caster (superfine) sugar

1   First, make the miso sauce. Combine all of the ingredients in a saucepan over low heat and cook until the sugar dissolves and the mixture thickens slightly. Take care, as the miso burns easily. Remove from the heat and set aside.

2   Preheat the oven to 180°C (350°F) and line a baking tray with baking paper.

3   Cut the eggplant into thick discs and salt them thoroughly, then place in a colander and leave for 15 minutes to draw out excess moisture.

4   Rinse the eggplant and thoroughly dry with paper towels, then coat the pieces in the oil. Place on the prepared tray and bake in the oven for 20 minutes, or until a knife inserted into the eggplant passes through easily.

5   Remove the eggplant from the oven and preheat the grill (broiler). Line a baking tray with foil and transfer the eggplant to it. Slather the top of each disc with the miso sauce and place under the grill for 1–2 minutes, or just long enough to brown the miso. Divide the eggplant among four plates and serve.

TENPURA ASPARA
TEMPURA ASPARAGUS

In addition to featuring five colours and five flavours, shōjin ryōri also follows the principle of five textures, one of which is tenpura, or frying – the other four being cutting, boiling, grilling (broiling) and steaming. In Japan, bitter but delicious sansai (wild mountain herbs) are used; these have a similar texture to asparagus, which we've chosen for this recipe.

**SERVES 4 AS PART OF
A SHŌJIN RYŌRI SET**

125 g (1 cup) Tempura flour
(page 219), plus extra to coat
250 ml (1 cup) cold water or
sparkling water
1 bunch asparagus
neutral oil, for deep-frying
lemon, to serve

1   Using chopsticks, mix the tempura flour with the water to make a batter – a slightly lumpy texture is preferable.

2   Snap off the tough, dry ends of the asparagus and discard. If the asparagus stalks are thicker than 1.5 cm (½ in) in diameter, you can peel them if you wish; this will result in a more tender exterior.

3   Fill a large, heavy-based saucepan one-third of the way with oil. Heat over medium heat to 180°C (350°F); a pinch of flour dropped into the oil should sizzle on contact.

4   Coat the asparagus in tempura flour, then dip into the batter. (If the flour doesn't adhere to the asparagus, dampen the stalks with a little water before coating in flour.) Deep-fry the asparagus for 2–3 minutes, until crispy. Transfer the fried asparagus to a wire rack or a plate lined with paper towels and season with salt. Serve with a squeeze of lemon.

Note
Any excess batter can be drizzled into the deep-frying oil to create crunchy batter pieces known as tenkasu. Tenkasu can be added to noodle dishes or Monjayaki (page 164) for texture.

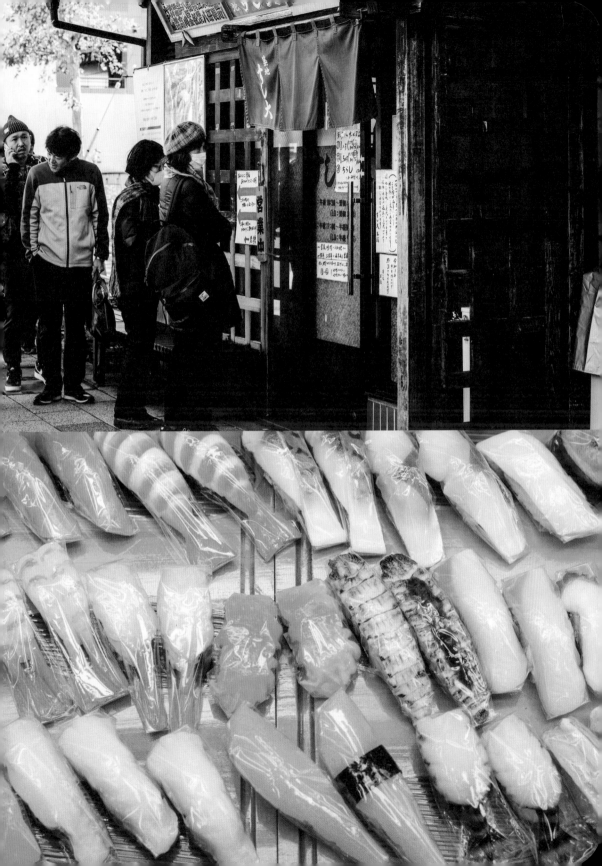

NIMONO

DASHI-SIMMERED VEGETABLES

Nimono means 'simmered things' in Japanese, and is a general term for all simmered dishes. Here, we use daikon (Japanese radish), taro, lotus root and firm tofu, a wonderful combination that soaks up the flavours of the dashi broth. Any vegetable suited to stewing, such as carrot, lotus root, pumpkin (winter squash) and potato, can be used.

**SERVES 4 AS PART OF
A SHŌJIN RYŌRI SET**

1 daikon (Japanese radish),
  cut into 2 cm (¾ in) lengths

1 handful of Japanese
  short-grain rice

200 ml (6¾ fl oz) Konbu dashi
  (page 221)

2 tablespoons sake

60 ml (¼ cup) soy sauce

3 tablespoons caster
  (superfine) sugar

1 tablespoon mirin

1 × 200 g (7 oz) block fried tofu,
  cut into bite-sized pieces

½ lotus root, cut into
  bite-sized pieces

250 g (9 oz) taro, cut into
  bite-sized pieces

100 g (3½ oz) snow peas
  (mangetout), stems
  and strings removed

1   Place the daikon and rice in a saucepan and cover with water. Bring to the boil over medium heat and cook for 20 minutes, or until the daikon is almost cooked (a knife inserted into a piece should pass through easily). Drain the daikon and discard the liquid and rice. This step removes any bitterness from the daikon.

2   In a clean saucepan, combine the konbu dashi, sake, soy sauce, sugar and mirin, then add the daikon, tofu, lotus root and taro. Cut out a circle of baking paper the same size as the mouth of the saucepan and place on top of the liquid; this will prevent it from evaporating too quickly. Simmer over medium-low heat until the daikon has taken on the flavour of the broth, approximately 30 minutes.

3   Meanwhile, fill a bowl with iced water. Bring a saucepan of water to the boil over high heat. Blanch the snow peas in the boiling water until they turn bright green, then drain and transfer to the iced water immediately until chilled. Drain well.

4   Divide the nimono among four bowls and garnish each one with the snow peas.

KŌN SURINAGASHI

SWEETCORN SOUP

Soup is very much a part of a Japanese meal, and while miso soup is the traditional offering, sweetcorn soup – served as corn potage or corn surinagashi – is incredibly popular. You will even find hot, ready-to-drink versions in vending machines! Frozen or tinned corn kernels can be used for this recipe, though it is best made in summer when corn is in season and naturally sweet.

**SERVES 4 AS PART OF
A SHŌJIN RYŌRI SET**

15 ml (½ fl oz) olive oil

1 onion, finely diced

400 g (2 cups) corn kernels

400 ml (13½ fl oz) Konbu dashi
   (page 221)

100 g (3 ½ oz) saikyo miso
   (see glossary)

400 ml (13½ fl oz) soy milk

sanshō (Japanese pepper),
   to serve

1   In a saucepan large enough to hold all of the ingredients, heat the olive oil over medium heat and fry the onion until soft but not coloured.

2   Add all of the ingredients, except the soy milk and sanshō, and bring to the boil. Skim away any impurities that rise to the surface and simmer for 10 minutes.

3   Add the soy milk and allow the soup to return to a simmer for a further 10 minutes, but do not let it boil – the soy milk will curdle! Remove from the heat and allow to cool slightly before blending with a hand-held blender, then return to low heat to keep warm.

4   Season with salt to taste and sprinkle with sanshō just before serving.

SORAMAME GOHAN

BROAD BEAN RICE

In kaiseki restaurants in Japan, there is usually a rice course, with the rice cooked in a large donabe (claypot) with seasonal ingredients. One of our favourites is soramame gohan, a spring dish in which the rice is cooked with sweet broad (fava) beans or edamame.

**SERVES 4 AS PART OF
A SHŌJIN RYŌRI SET**

1 tablespoon salt, plus extra

250 ml (1 cup) Konbu dashi
   (page 221), chilled

1 kg (2 lb 3 oz) broad (fava) beans
   or 250 g (9 oz) edamame,
   outer pods removed

rice, to serve

1   Combine the salt with the konbu dashi and set aside in a container in the fridge.

2   Fill a large bowl with iced water. Bring a large saucepan of water to the boil over high heat and lightly salt the water. Blanch the beans in the boiling water for 1 minute, then drain and transfer to the iced water immediately until chilled.

3   If using broad beans, remove the pale inner skin of the beans and discard. Place the beans in the salted dashi, which will lightly season the beans and help them keep their colour. Refrigerate the beans in the dashi until ready to serve.

4   To serve, divide the rice among four bowls. Drain the beans and top each bowl with 2 tablespoons of the beans.

KONBINI

A Japanese convenience store. A far superior specimen to any of its international counterparts.

Tokyoites all have a favourite konbini. Is it 7-Eleven, Family Mart or Lawson? Who does a better karaage (fried chicken)? Which konbini has the latest seasonal special? Who is unveiling a series of limited-edition themed snacks in partnership with a manga or anime studio?

Konbini first emerged in Japan in the 1970s, brought to the country by American-owned group 7-Eleven (Japanese company Seven & I Holdings is the current parent company of 7-Eleven Japan). In the Japanese spirit, they transformed konbini into an indispensable part of Japanese culture.

Manga in the magazine aisle? Check. Samurai-style face masks? Check. Emergency shirt? Check. False eyelashes? Check. (Why this would necessitate an emergency trip to the konbini is anyone's guess.)

But the crowning glory is the sheer variety of food in the konbini. It is possible to live solely off this, and even pull together a multi-course konbini dinner.

There are the staples: bentō, an array of instant ramen, packets of soups and rice porridge (just ask and they'll add hot water or heat it up in the microwave). There are individually packed onsen tamago (hot-spring eggs) and ajitama (soy-seasoned eggs) in the fridge, ready to heat up and pop onto your rice or in your ramen if you feel like it.

In autumn and winter, there is a bubbling vat of oden, a Japanese stew where you can pick from simmered sides including daikon (Japanese radish), shirataki (konjac) noodles, hard-boiled eggs, tofu stuffed with mochi, and a variety of fishcakes.

There's snack food, from savoury options such as nikuman (steamed meat buns), yakisoba pan (bread rolls stuffed with noodles), sandwiches and crisp, nori-wrapped triangles of onigiri (rice balls), to sweet items like fluffy buns filled with custard, cream or red bean. And we haven't yet considered the potechi (potato chips/crisps), which range from tame flavours such as nori, shōyu (soy sauce), mentaiko (spicy pollock roe) and wasabi beef, to more adventurous creations such as ramen, mandarin (yes, the fruit), uni (sea urchin) and wagyu beef sandwich.

Look into the fridge and freezer and you'll see wobbly creme caramel purin (puddings) and seasonal ice cream impossible to find outside of Japan (chestnut, purple sweet potato, mochi!). The candy aisle is filled with curiously named sweets: soft chocolates called Meltykiss and Crunky; more flavours of Pocky than you can imagine; satisfyingly salty umeboshi (pickled plum) gummies in summer (to replenish the body's electrolytes); and Milky, a soft condensed milk sweet featuring mascot Peko-chan.

There are refreshing bottles of green, roasted, oolong, royal milk and black teas, a heated cabinet stocked with tins of hot chocolate and coffee, and an alcohol section with beer, shochu and sake.

In a country where there are commemorative days for roll cakes, hotcakes, dorayaki and ehomaki (large rolls of sushi), the konbini are also the place to find limited-edition treats.

CHIKIN KARAAGE

MARINATED FRIED CHICKEN

It is hard to resist the allure of a karaage street stall, especially on a cold spring, autumn or winter's day, when the scent of fried chicken wafts through the air and the sizzle can be heard from down the street.

We're huddled around the tachi (standing) area of a karaage stall in Ameyokochō as the owner quickly fries up our order and hands it to us in a paper box. 'Dōzo,' he says, gesturing to an array of sauces. But there is little need for those. The crisp chicken pieces taste wonderful on their own, succulent and juicy, with a little saltiness from the soy.

SERVES 4

600 g (1 lb 5 oz) boneless chicken thighs, skin on, cut into bite-sized pieces

100 ml (3½ fl oz) soy sauce

30 ml (1 fl oz) sake

1 garlic clove, finely chopped

1 × 3 cm (1¼ in) piece ginger, grated

75 g (2¾ oz) cornflour (corn starch)

150 g (5½ oz) potato starch

neutral oil, for deep-frying

mayonnaise (preferably Kewpie) and lemon wedges, to serve

1   In a large, non-reactive bowl, combine the chicken, soy sauce, sake, garlic and ginger. Massage everything together and place in the fridge to marinate for 20 minutes.

2   Combine the cornflour and potato starch in a large mixing bowl. Drain the chicken, then coat in the combined starches.

3   Fill a large, heavy-based saucepan one-third of the way with oil. Heat over medium heat to 180°C (350°F); a pinch of flour dropped into the oil should sizzle on contact. Deep-fry the chicken, working in batches if necessary, for 3–4 minutes, or until golden brown and cooked through. Transfer to a rack to drain and season with salt.

4   Serve the chikin karaage immediately with mayonnaise and lemon wedges. Alternatively, you can leave it to cool on the rack and pack it in a bentō for the next day.

TORI NANBAN

FRIED CHICKEN WITH TARTARE SAUCE

Tori nanban hails from Miyazaki Prefecture on the island of Kyushu in Japan's south, but has since become a popular dish served throughout the country. A yōshoku (Western-style) creation, it is said to be inspired by nanbanzuke (vinegar-marinated fried fish, a Japanese version of the Portuguese escabeche) with the crispy, deep-fried pieces of chicken tossed quickly in a tangy, salty sauce. It is then topped with a creamy blend of mayo, boiled egg and cornichons, and is irresistible when eaten piping hot.

SERVES 4

150 g (1 cup) plain (all-purpose) flour

1 teaspoon salt, plus extra to taste

½ teaspoon freshly ground black pepper, plus extra to taste

500 g (1 lb 2 oz) skinless, boneless chicken thighs, cut into bite-sized pieces

2 eggs, beaten

125 ml (½ cup) neutral oil, for frying

100 g (3½ oz) mixed salad leaves

1 quantity Basic salad dressing (page 225)

Nanban tare

2 tablespoons soy sauce

2 tablespoons rice vinegar

1 teaspoon caster (superfine) sugar

1 teaspoon salt

Tartare sauce

½ onion, chopped

1 boiled egg, peeled and chopped

4 cornichons, chopped

3 tablespoons mayonnaise (preferably Kewpie)

1 tablespoon lemon juice

1 Combine all of the nanban tare ingredients in a small saucepan over low heat and bring to a simmer to dissolve the sugar and salt. Transfer to a large mixing bowl or container and set aside.

2 To make the tartare sauce, soak the chopped onion in water for 5 minutes, then drain, thoroughly dry with paper towels, and combine with the remaining ingredients. Season with salt and pepper to taste and set aside in the fridge until required.

3 In a large mixing bowl, whisk together the flour, salt and pepper. Coat the chicken in the flour mixture, dust off any excess, then dip in the beaten eggs.

4 Heat the oil in a large, heavy-based frying pan over medium heat until the temperature reaches 180°C (350°F); a pinch of flour dropped into the oil should sizzle on contact. Working in batches to avoid overcrowding if necessary, fry the chicken until golden brown on both sides, approximately 3 minutes each side. Remove the chicken from the pan and keep warm; the oil can be reserved for reuse another time.

5 Dress the mixed salad leaves with the salad dressing.

6 Toss the cooked chicken through the tare to coat, then place on a serving dish. Top with the tartare sauce and serve with the salad.

KATSU BĀGĀ

KASTU BURGER

The filling for this katsu burger is menchi katsu, a deep-fried minced (ground) meat and onion patty that was first created at a yōshoku (Western-style) restaurant in Tokyo during the Meiji era (1868–1912). The panko coating keeps the juiciness of the minced meat in, with fragrant onion and crisp cabbage accentuating the texture and flavour. The burger itself is quick to make, though the patties need to be frozen for 1–2 hours in advance.

In Japan, keep a look out for menchi katsu in butchers, often found in shotengai (neighbourhood shopping streets). They sell the delicious fried patties and croquettes piping hot and ready to eat (just be sure to stay in the seating area of the stall while eating; walking and eating is considered impolite).

SERVES 4

½ onion, finely chopped

75 g (1 cup) finely chopped cabbage, plus ¼ cabbage, finely shredded

1 tablespoon salt, plus extra to taste

300 g (10½ oz) minced (ground) beef (30% fat is recommended)

60 g (1 cup) plus 2 tablespoons panko breadcrumbs

3 eggs

1 tablespoon milk

150 g (1 cup) plain (all-purpose) flour

neutral oil, for deep-frying

4 Milk bread rolls (page 216) or store-bought burger buns

mayonnaise, to serve

1   To make the burger sauce, combine the mirin and sake in a large saucepan and bring to the boil over medium–high heat. Boil until the aroma of alcohol has dissipated or the liquid is reduced by half, then add the remaining ingredients, along with 100 ml (3½ fl oz) of water and cook, stirring, until the sugar and miso dissolve. Remove from the heat and allow to cool before storing in an airtight container in the fridge, where the sauce will keep for up to 1 month.

2   Combine the onion and cabbage with the salt and place in a colander for 10 minutes to draw out water. Squeeze out the excess liquid and transfer the vegetables to a large mixing bowl.

3   Mix in the minced beef, 2 tablespoons of the panko and 1 egg until well incorporated, then season with salt and pepper. Divide the mixture into four patties and place on a lined baking tray. Freeze the patties for 1–2 hours to set their shape and make them easier to crumb.

4   To create the crumbing mixture, whisk the milk and the remaining eggs in a bowl until homogenous. Place the flour on a large plate, season with salt and pepper and stir to combine. Place the remaining panko on a separate plate and line a third plate with baking paper.

5   Take a patty and coat it in the seasoned flour. Brush off any excess and dip the patty in the egg mixture, followed by the panko, making sure the patty is well coated in breadcrumbs. Transfer to the lined plate and repeat with the remaining patties, then place in the fridge until you are ready to fry.

6   Fill a large, heavy-based saucepan one-third of the way with oil. Heat over medium heat until small bubbles form on

Burger sauce

200 ml (6¾ fl oz) mirin

150 ml (5 fl oz) sake

100 g (3½ oz) tomato ketchup

150 g (5½ oz) hatchōmiso
(see glossary)

100 g (3½ oz) oyster sauce

100 g (3½ oz) caster
(superfine) sugar

150 g (5½ oz) akamiso
(red miso paste)

40 g (1½ oz) dijon mustard

the surface of a wooden chopstick inserted into the oil – approximately 160°C (320°F). Deep-fry the patties for 5 minutes each and drain on a rack.

7   Split the burger buns in half and toast in a toaster or under the grill (broiler).

8   To assemble, lay the four bottom buns out on a clean work surface. Place a patty on each of the bottom buns and top with the burger sauce, remaining cabbage and mayonnaise. Finish with the top bun and serve immediately.

YAKISOBA PAN

YAKISOBA ROLLS

Yakisoba pan is a quirky Japanese creation consisting of fried noodles stuffed in bread, specifically a hot dog roll or milk bun. The story goes that a customer of Nozawaya in Tokyo asked for the combination in the 1950s, and the invention has lined the shelves of Japanese bakeries and konbini (convenience stores) ever since.

SERVES 4

4 Milk bread rolls (page 216) or store-bought mini hot dog rolls

1 tablespoon unsalted butter or margarine, softened

300 g (10½ oz) Fried noodles (page 99)

beni shōga (pickled ginger), sliced, to serve

1 Split the bread rolls in half and spread with the butter. Divide the fried noodles between the rolls and top with lots of beni shōga. Serve immediately (though it also tastes fine cold).

NAPORITAN PAN

NAPOLETANA ROLLS

This is a twist on the Yakisoba roll (above), this time featuring spaghetti napoletana, a yōshoku (Western-style) favourite in Japan.

SERVES 4

4 Milk bread rolls (page 216) or store-bought mini hot dog rolls

1 tablespoon unsalted butter or margarine, softened

200 g (7 oz) dried spaghetti

1 tablespoon olive oil

½ onion, finely chopped

1 garlic clove, finely sliced

125 ml (½ cup) tomato ketchup

125 ml (½ cup) tomato passata (pureed tomatoes)

chopped parsley, to garnish

1 Split the bread rolls in half and spread with the butter. Meanwhile, cook the pasta according to the instructions on the packet, then drain.

2 Heat the olive oil in a large frying pan over medium heat, then add the onion and garlic and cook until soft. Stir in the ketchup and passata. Add the cooked spaghetti to the frying pan and mix well. Divide the spaghetti napoletana between the rolls and top with parsley.

Note
The napoletana rolls can be – and are usually – served cold.

BĪFU SHICHŪ HOTTO SANDO

BEEF STEW JAFFLES

In Asakusa, just off Nakamise – the main shopping strip leading up to Sensōji Temple – is Zero Food & Drink, a tiny little shop set up by a former sashimi chef. The specialty is grilled sandwiches, or jaffles, and this recipe (which uses a Japanese-style beef stew) is inspired by the house-made corned beef, which goes brilliantly with their house-made ginger ale.

SERVES 4

400 g (14 oz) Beef stew (page 66)

8 slices thick-cut white bread

4 slices cheese such as mozzarella, cheddar or gruyere

4 tablespoons chopped Japanese pickles (pages 18-25), preferably onions and cucumbers

1   Separate the beef pieces from the rest of the stew and shred them, then stir them back into the stew.

2   To assemble the jaffles, lay four pieces of bread out on a clean work surface. Place a slice of cheese on top of each piece of bread, followed by a generous spoonful of the stew, then the pickles and the remaining bread. Cook in a jaffle iron or sandwich press until the outside is crispy, the cheese has melted and the stew is heated through.

KARĒPAN
CURRY BUNS

The Japanese have a love affair with karēpan, curry stuffed in a bun, which is then baked or fried until golden brown. The bread first made its debut in 1927 and is still so favoured today it has a karēpan festival and a karēpan Grand Prix of its own.

Karēpan is typically filled with Japanese curry or Keema curry (page 64) as well as a soft-boiled egg that is buried within like a hidden treasure. The ones at Le Pain de Joël Robuchon, which also include vegetables like our recipe here, are our favourite.

**MAKES 8 SMALL OR
4 LARGE BUNS**

250 g (9 oz) cold Keema curry (page 64)

50 g (1¾ oz) cooked vegetables such as pumpkin (winter squash), potato or eggplant (aubergine), cut into pea-sized pieces

4 small soft-boiled eggs (optional)

neutral oil, for deep-frying

60 g (1 cup) panko breadcrumbs

Dough

150 ml (5½ oz) warm water

3 g (⅛ oz) instant yeast

250 g (1⅓ cups) plain (all-purpose) flour

10 g (¼ oz) caster (superfine) sugar

3 g (⅛ oz) salt

10 g (¼ oz) unsalted butter, at room temperature

1   To make the dough, combine the water and yeast in a large mixing bowl and leave for 10 minutes, or until the mixture starts to foam. Add the remaining ingredients and knead by hand or with a stand mixer fitted with a dough hook until you have a smooth and elastic dough.

2   Transfer the dough to a clean, lightly oiled bowl, cover with plastic wrap and set aside to rest in a warm place for 1–2 hours, or until doubled in size.

3   Use the palms of your hands to press down and deflate the dough, then divide it into eight evenly sized balls, or four if you are using soft-boiled eggs. Flatten the balls out and evenly divide the curry, vegetables and eggs (if using) between them. Enclose the filling by pinching the edges of the dough together, then form the filled dough into balls.

4   Fill a large, heavy-based saucepan one-third of the way with oil. Heat over medium heat until small bubbles form on the surface of a wooden chopstick inserted into the oil – approximately 165°C (330°F).

5   Lightly dampen the outside of the buns with water by patting them with wet hands or spritzing them, then sprinkle with the panko.

6   Deep-fry the buns in batches until golden brown, then place on a rack to drain. The karēpan can be eaten immediately or cooled and refrigerated, to be reheated later in a 180°C (350°F) oven for 10 minutes.

MATCHA CHOUX

※

Choux puffs filled with cream are not a Japanese creation, but they are wildly popular in Tokyo, where cream puff stands make the crisp shells with fillings such as vanilla, custard, caramel, chocolate and matcha to order. There is always a seasonal filling as well: in spring, this might be strawberry; in summer, agrum; and in autumn, mont blanc.

MAKES 9 × 7.5 CM (3 IN) CHOUX PUFFS

40 g (1½ oz) unsalted butter

60 ml (¼ cup) milk

50 g (⅓ cup) plain (all-purpose) flour

small pinch of salt

2 eggs, beaten

Creme patissiere

4 egg yolks

60 g (2 oz) caster (superfine) sugar

50 g (1¾ oz) cornflour (corn starch) or custard powder

10 g (¼ oz) matcha (green tea powder)

300 ml (10¼ fl oz) milk

½ teaspoon vanilla bean paste

200 ml (6¾ fl oz) cream (minimum 35% milk fat)

1   First, make the creme patissiere. In a large mixing bowl, whisk the egg yolks and sugar together until pale and creamy. Add the cornflour and matcha and stir to combine well.

2   In a small saucepan over low heat, bring the milk and vanilla bean paste to the boil. When just boiling, remove from the heat and slowly pour the milk into the egg mixture in a thin stream, whisking constantly. Don't pour too quickly, or you will cook the eggs.

3   Pour the egg mixture into the saucepan and cook, stirring constantly, over medium heat until it is between 70°C (160°F) and 80°C (175°F), or until thickened and a line drawn through the mixture with the back of a spoon remains. Remove from the heat and transfer to a bowl, then press a piece of plastic wrap onto the surface of the mixture. Allow to cool to room temperature, then set aside in the fridge.

4   Next, make the cookie. Place the butter and sugar in the bowl of a stand mixer fitted with a paddle attachment and beat until pale and fluffy. Add the flour and cinnamon and beat until just combined. Sandwich the batter between two pieces of baking paper and roll out to a thickness of 2–3 mm (⅛ in). Freeze until required.

5   Preheat the oven to 190°C (375°F) and line a baking tray with baking paper.

6   Combine the butter, milk and 60 ml (¼ cup) of water in a saucepan over medium heat. Bring to a simmer and add the flour and salt, stirring constantly until the mixture comes together in a ball.

7   Remove from the heat and slowly add the beaten egg one-quarter at a time, incorporating well after each addition.

8   Transfer the mixture to a piping bag fitted with a plain nozzle and pipe 9 × 5 cm (2 in) mounds onto the lined baking tray, leaving enough space for the dough to expand by half.

Cookie

50 g (1¾ oz) unsalted butter

40 g (1½ oz) caster (superfine) sugar

50 g (⅓ cup) plain (all-purpose) flour

½ teaspoon ground cinnamon

9   Remove the cookie dough from the freezer. Using a 5 cm (2 in) round cookie cutter, cut nine circles out of the frozen cookie dough. Place a round of cookie dough onto each choux mound.

10 Bake the choux puffs for 20 minutes, then reduce the heat to 170°C (340°F) and bake for a further 20 minutes. Remove the choux puffs from the oven and transfer to a wire rack to cool.

11 Meanwhile, remove the creme patissiere from the fridge. In the bowl of a stand mixer fitted with a whisk attachment, whip the cream to stiff peaks. Press the refrigerated mixture through a sieve to make it as smooth as possible, then fold through the cream. Transfer to a piping bag with a small, round nozzle and return to the fridge. The cream will get thicker as it rests.

12 Once the choux puffs are cool, poke a hole in the bottom of each one using the piping bag nozzle and pipe in the creme patissiere. Serve immediately.

BAKED CHEESE TARTS

Lines can often be found outside Japan's baked cheese tart shops, which are filled with rows of mini pastries with golden shells and an oozy cheese filling. The tarts are baked in small batches, meaning customers get to enjoy them fresh from the oven and piping hot.

MAKES 2 × 15 CM (6 IN) TARTS OR 20 × 5 CM (2 IN) TARTS

10 g (¼ oz) unsalted butter

50 g (1¾ oz) caster (superfine) sugar

120 g (4¼ oz) cream cheese

1 egg

15 g (½ oz) plain (all-purpose) flour

120 g (4¼ oz) double (heavy) cream (minimum 48% milk fat)

Shortcrust pastry

100 g (3½ oz) cold unsalted butter, diced

200 g (1⅓ cups) plain (all-purpose) flour, plus extra for dusting

1 tablespoon caster (superfine) sugar

1 teaspoon salt

1 egg yolk

2 tablespoons iced water

Note
You can glaze the tarts with apricot or yuzu jam. Refrigerate the tarts for 2 hours, then follow the glazing instructions on page 134.

1   To make the pastry, in a large mixing bowl, use your fingertips to rub the butter into the flour until the mixture resembles breadcrumbs. Mix the sugar, salt and egg yolk into the flour mixture, then add the water and knead briefly until it comes together as a smooth dough. Take care not to overwork the dough, as this will result in a tougher pastry that shrinks when baked. Flatten the dough into a disc, cover with plastic wrap and refrigerate for 2–3 hours.

2   Dust the pastry with a little flour and roll out to a thickness of 3 mm (⅛ in). Line two 15 cm (6 in) tart tins or 20 × 5 cm (2 in) tartlet tins with the pastry, pressing into place where the sides and base meet. Cover and set aside to rest in the fridge for 30 minutes.

3   Meanwhile, make the filling. In a stand mixer fitted with a paddle attachment, beat together the butter, sugar and cream cheese on medium speed until smooth. Add the egg and continue beating until it is fully incorporated.

4   Scrape down the side of the mixer and sift in the flour. Beat on medium until smooth, then transfer the mixture to a clean bowl. Wash the bowl of the stand mixer.

5   Fit the whisk attachment to the stand mixer and add the cream to the bowl. Whip the cream until it is light and fluffy and retains its shape when the whisk is lifted. Fold the cream into the cream cheese mixture and transfer the filling to a piping bag fitted with a plain nozzle.

6   Preheat the oven to 200°C (400°F). Prick the bases of the tarts with a fork. Line each tart with a piece of baking paper and fill with baking weights, dried beans or uncooked rice. Blind-bake the tart cases for 10 minutes. Remove the weights and baking paper and bake the tart cases for an additional 5 minutes, or until golden. Remove from the oven and cool.

7   Reduce the oven temperature to 170°C (340°F) if making two large tarts, or leave at 200°C (400°F) if making small tarts.

8   Fill the tarts with the cream cheese filling. For large tarts, bake the filled tarts for 20 minutes; for small tarts, bake the filled tarts for 7 minutes. Remove from the oven and allow to rest for 15 minutes before consuming.

SATSUMA-IMO TARUTO

SWEET POTATO TART

Just half an hour from central Tokyo is Kawagoe, a town known for its 'Little Edo' main street. Kawagoe prospered during the Edo Period (1603–1868), when it served as a supplier of commodities to the capital, Edo. The kurazukuri (clay-walled merchant houses) that line the township are a legacy of this history.

Kawagoe escaped the damage that ravaged Tokyo during the Great Kantō Earthquake of 1923, and emerged almost unscathed from World War II, making it one of the rare areas near Tokyo with buildings preserved from the 18th and 19th centuries. A stroll down the main street feels like a step back in time, particularly in Kashiya Yokochō, or Penny Candy Alley, where Shōwa-era (1926–1989) dagashiya (candy shops) line the narrow path, filled with nostalgic candy, old-fashioned toys and Kawagoe's specialty: satsuma-imo (purple sweet potato).

Purple sweet potato is everywhere: sold simply roasted to enjoy in its sweet, natural glory; as chips (crisps); and in purin (puddings), sofuto kurimu (soft-serve ice cream), kakigori (shaved ice) and beer (craft brewery Coedo hails from the Saitama region, and the locals of Kawagoe are notably proud of it). This recipe for sweet potato tart was inspired by our travels there; the purple sweet potato makes a delicious, not-too-sweet filling.

**MAKES 2 × 15 CM (6 IN) TARTS
OR 20 × 5 CM (2 IN) TARTS**

350 g (12½ oz) purple sweet
potato, unpeeled

1 teaspoon ground nutmeg

50 g (1¾ oz) caster
(superfine) sugar

20 g (¾ oz) unsalted butter,
at room temperature

120 ml (4½ fl oz) cream

1 egg, plus 1 egg yolk

1 tablespoon milk

1 quantity Creme patissiere
(page 128), cream and
matcha omitted

1 tablespoon apricot jam

whipped cream, to serve

Shortcrust pastry

100 g (3½ oz) cold unsalted
butter, diced

200 g (1⅓ cups) cake flour,
plus extra for dusting

1 tablespoon caster
(superfine) sugar

1 teaspoon salt

1 egg yolk

2 tablespoons iced water

1   To make the pastry, in a large mixing bowl, use your fingertips to rub the butter into the flour until the mixture resembles breadcrumbs. Mix the sugar, salt and egg yolk into the flour mixture, then add the water and knead briefly until it comes together as a smooth dough. Take care not to overwork the dough, as this will result in a tougher pastry that shrinks when baked. Flatten the dough into a disc, cover with plastic wrap and refrigerate for 2–3 hours.

2   Meanwhile, prepare the sweet potato. Cut the sweet potato into two even pieces and place in a large saucepan. Cover with cold water, bring to the boil over medium–high heat and cook until the sweet potato is very soft. Drain in a colander and leave for 10 minutes to cool and dry. Peel away the skin and discard, then place the sweet potato in a sieve and press the flesh through to get a very smooth puree. You should be left with approximately 300 g (10½ oz). Transfer to a large mixing bowl and set aside.

3   Dust the pastry with a little flour and roll out to a thickness of 3 mm (⅛ in). Line two 15 cm (6 in) tart tins or 20 × 5 cm (2 in) tartlet tins with the pastry, pressing into place where the sides and base meet. Cover and set aside to rest in the fridge for 30 minutes.

4   Preheat the oven to 200°C (400°F). Prick the bases of the tarts with a fork. Line each tart with a piece of baking paper and fill with baking weights, dried beans or uncooked rice. Blind-bake the tart cases for 10 minutes. Remove the weights and baking paper and bake the tart cases for an additional 5 minutes, or until golden. Remove from the oven and cool.

5   Add the nutmeg, sugar, butter, cream and egg yolk to the sweet potato puree and mix well to combine, then transfer to a piping bag fitted with a wide nozzle.

6   Whisk the milk and remaining egg together in a small bowl. Spread or pipe the creme patissiere onto the bottom of the tart shells and bake in the oven for 5 minutes to set the top. Remove the tarts from the oven and pipe on the sweet potato mixture, smoothing out the top if desired. Brush the tarts with the egg mixture and bake for a further 10 minutes, or until browned. Remove from the oven and allow to cool.

7   Combine the apricot jam and 1 tablespoon of water in a small saucepan over medium heat and simmer for long enough to dissolve the jam. Brush the tarts with jam to glaze and serve with whipped cream.

SUFURE CHĪZUKĒKI

COTTON SOFT CHEESECAKE

Cotton soft cheesecakes (or souffle cheesecakes as they are known in Japan) are light, soft and fluffy, with a citrusy tang from lemon juice and yuzu jam. This was the most popular dessert at our Japanese restaurant, and is achievable as long as you pay close attention to timing – otherwise the cake will crack! While it might be tempting to eat it right away, it is best chilled overnight, as the fresh cake will be too crumbly.

SERVES 8–12

neutral oil, for greasing

70 g (2½ oz) caster (superfine) sugar, plus extra for dusting

200 g (7 oz) milk

200 g (7 oz) cream cheese

120 g (4¼ oz) egg whites (from approximately 3 eggs)

80 g (2¾ oz) egg yolks (from approximately 5 eggs)

10 g (¼ oz) cornflour (corn starch)

40 g (1½ oz) plain (all-purpose) flour

20 g (¾ oz) lemon juice (from approximately ½ lemon)

1 tablespoon yuzu jam (see glossary) or orange marmalade, to glaze

1   Preheat the oven to 165°C (330°F) and line a greased 16 cm (6¼ in) round cake tin with baking paper. Grease the inside of the paper and dust the walls with sugar. Put the kettle or a large saucepan of water on to boil.

2   Heat the milk and cream cheese in a small saucepan over low heat and whisk until homogenous. Remove from the heat and set aside to cool to room temperature.

3   In the bowl of a stand mixer fitted with a whisk attachment, beat the egg whites until soft peaks form, then slowly add 50 g (1¾ oz) of the sugar, whisking continuously until the sugar dissolves and stiff peaks form.

4   Transfer the cooled cream cheese mixture to a large mixing bowl and add the egg yolks, whisking to combine. Repeat the process with the remaining 20 g (¾ oz) of sugar, followed by the cornflour, the flour and finally the lemon juice, in that order, whisking to combine after each addition. Gently fold the mixture into the egg whites, then pour into the lined cake tin.

5   Place the cake tin into a baking tin and transfer to the oven. Very carefully pour boiling water into the baking tin until it reaches halfway up the sides of the cake tin. Bake the cake in the water bath for 20 minutes, then reduce the temperature to 110°C (230°F) and bake for a further 40 minutes. You can remove the cake from the oven now, but for a brown top, increase the temperature to 180°C (350°F) and bake for a further 10 minutes, or until browned to your liking.

6   Remove the cake from the water bath and leave to cool to room temperature before turning out and placing on a cake rack.

7   In a small saucepan, heat the yuzu jam over low heat until it thins. Brush the cake with the yuzu jam to glaze. Once the glaze has set, cover the cake and refrigerate overnight.

PURIN À LA MODE

The Japanese purin is a softer, wobblier version of creme caramel, with stores dedicated entirely to the sweet, creamy dessert. Some feature milk or cream from Hokkaido or eggs from Hyōgo or Iwate, with regional variations including matcha, hōjicha (roasted green tea) and sake.

Purin à la mode was first introduced by grand chef S. Weil of the Hotel New Grand in Yokohama in the 1920s, and to this day, it is still a staple in kissaten (traditional coffee shops), served with whipped cream, a liqueur-soaked cherry, apples cut into the shape of an usagi (rabbit) or candied nuts.

Here, we pair it with more traditional flavours and dango (glutinous rice balls).

SERVES 6

neutral oil, for greasing

140 g (5 oz) caster (superfine) sugar

160 ml (5½ fl oz) milk

70 ml (2¼ fl oz) cream (minimum 35% milk fat)

½ teaspoon vanilla bean paste

2 eggs

Red bean paste (page 143), to serve

seasonal fruits, to serve

whipped cream, to serve (optional)

1   Preheat the oven to 150°C (300°F). Grease six 100 ml (3½ fl oz) heatproof dariole moulds with oil and set aside.

2   Place 80 g (2¾ oz) of the sugar in a small saucepan over medium heat and cook until it melts and begins to bubble. Reduce the heat to low and continue cooking until it turns nut brown. Remove from the heat and quickly but carefully add 20 ml (¾ fl oz) of water, swirling the pan to combine, then divide the caramel between the darioles. Transfer the darioles to the fridge to set.

3   In a clean saucepan, bring the milk, cream and vanilla bean paste to a simmer over low heat. Meanwhile, in a mixing bowl, whisk the egg yolks and remaining sugar together until pale and creamy. Slowly pour the milk mixture into the egg mixture in a thin stream, whisking constantly. Don't pour too quickly, or you'll cook the eggs.

4   Strain the mixture into a pitcher and skim the foam off the top. Cover with plastic wrap and set aside to cool in the fridge.

5   Put a kettle or a large saucepan of water on to boil and place the darioles into a baking tin. Divide the milk mixture between the darioles and cover with heatproof plastic wrap. Very carefully pour boiling water into the baking tin until it reaches halfway up the sides of the darioles.

6   Cover the baking tin with foil and place in the oven, taking care not to spill the water. Bake for 15 minutes, then carefully remove the foil (hot steam will be released) and check if the puddings are set.

Dango

100 g (3½ oz) glutinous
    rice flour
10 g (¼ oz) icing
    (confectioners') sugar

7   If not set, replace the foil and return the puddings to the oven for 3 minutes. Continue cooking and checking in 3 minute intervals until the puddings are set.

8   Remove the puddings from the water, cool to room temperature and refrigerate until required.

9   To make the dango, fill a large bowl with iced water and bring a large saucepan of water to the boil over high heat. In a mixing bowl, combine the glutinous rice flour and icing sugar. Slowly add 100 ml (3½ fl oz) of water until it comes together as a dough; you may not need all of the water.

10   Shape the dough into balls 2 cm (¾ in) in diameter. Carefully place the balls into the boiling water and cook until they begin to float. Remove the dango from the saucepan using a slotted spoon and immediately transfer to the iced water. Keep in iced water until required.

11   To serve, turn the puddings out onto individual plates. Drain the dango and divide them between the plates, then top with red bean paste, fruit and whipped cream (if using).

CHOC–ORANGE POUND CAKE

Peruse any French–Japanese bakery or patisserie in Japan and you will likely come across perfectly baked loaves of pound cake in the traditional flavours of chocolate, choc-orange and matcha. In Tokyo and Yokahama, there is even a dedicated mini-pound cake patisserie with beautifully glazed confections sprinkled with freeze-dried strawberries, glistening fruits of the forest and vibrant orange slices. This rich pound cake is a blend of chocolate and orange, accentuated with Grand Marnier.

SERVES 8–12

neutral oil, for greasing

110 g (4 oz) unsalted butter, at room temperature

½ teaspoon vanilla bean paste

130 g (4½ oz) caster (superfine) sugar

2 eggs, separated

20 ml (¾ fl oz) orange juice

15 g (½ oz) Dutch (unsweetened) cocoa powder

¾ teaspoon baking powder

25 g (1 oz) almond flour

75 g (½ cup) plain (all-purpose) flour

35 g (1¼ oz) candied orange slices, chopped

100 g (3½ oz) milk or dark chocolate, roughly chopped

20 ml (¾ fl oz) Grand Marnier or other orange liqueur

To decorate

40 g (⅓ cup) icing (confectioners') sugar

10 g (¼ oz) Dutch (unsweetened) cocoa powder

15 g (½ oz) unsalted butter, melted

1 tablespoon warm milk

20 g (¾ oz) candied orange slices

2 tablespoons edible chocolate pearls

1   Preheat the oven to 180°C (350°F) and line a greased 18 cm × 8 cm × 6 cm (7 in × 3 in × 2½ in) loaf tin with baking paper.

2   Using a stand mixer fitted with a paddle attachment, beat together the butter, vanilla bean paste and 50 g (1¾ oz) of the sugar until pale and fluffy. Add the egg yolks and orange juice and combine. Transfer the mixture to a large mixing bowl and thoroughly clean and dry the bowl of the stand mixer. Affix the whisk attachment.

3   Whisk together the egg whites and 60 g (2 oz) of the sugar until stiff peaks form.

4   Meanwhile, sift the cocoa powder into the butter mixture and fold it in with a spatula. Repeat with the baking powder, followed by the almond flour and then the plain flour, folding the mixture together after each addition.

5   Finally, fold the egg whites into the mixture, followed by the candied orange and chocolate, taking care not to overmix. Pour into the pound cake tin, smoothing out the surface but making the sides of the mixture higher than the centre (the cake will rise in the centre).

6   Bake for 40 minutes, or until a skewer inserted into the centre of the cake comes out clean. Transfer to a wire rack and allow to cool in its tin for 15 minutes, then turn out.

7   In a small saucepan over medium heat, mix together the remaining 20 g (¾ oz) of the sugar and the Grand Marnier. Cook until the sugar dissolves, then brush the mixture over the cake. Wrap in plastic wrap until cool.

8   To decorate, sift together the icing sugar and cocoa powder. Add the butter and milk and whisk to combine; the mixture should be the consistency of thin cream. (You can add more milk if necessary to achieve the desired consistency.) Drizzle the mixture over the cooled cake, then decorate with the candied orange and chocolate pearls.

WAGASHI

Japan's traditional sweet, made with anko (red bean paste) and shiroan (white bean paste).

It is winter in Kanazawa, and the rain is pelting down outside. For the moment, however, it doesn't matter, as we are comfortably nestled by the window of Morihachi Honten, gazing upon the tranquil setting of a beautiful Japanese garden. We've chosen our wagashi (how do you choose when they all look so pretty?), which comes served with a bowl of velvety, grassy, bittersweet matcha.

After this, we'll peruse the Kanazawa Museum of Wooden Japanese Sweets Moulds, an incredible display of intricately carved wooden moulds and branding irons known as yaki-in from the Edo period to the Shōwa period (1603–1989). There are thousands of them, from moulds in the shape of Kaga's plum-blossom crest, to moulds for the shōgun, and moulds depicting delicate flowers, birds, cranes and fish. The teahouse and museum are all housed within the same Edo-era structure, so the Shinto gods can rain down on this little patch as much as they wish.

Morihachi was established in 1625 as the purveyor of wagashi to the Maeda clan, the historical rulers of Kanazawa and the surrounding Kaga Domain, and continues to create some of the country's most exquisite confectioneries. A Tokyo equivalent is Toraya, founded in the late Muromachi period (1336–1573), which has provided sweets to the Imperial Family since 1586. Toraya has shops throughout Tokyo, housed in tiny, traditional machiya, as well as sleek, modern spaces designed by Tadao Ando and Naito Architects & Associates (their all-white Tokyo Midtown shop in Roppongi is a striking architectural masterpiece).

Despite the influx of French-style patisseries, wagashi still remains deeply entrenched in Japan's culinary scene. Gardens, temple grounds and historical houses will almost always have a teahouse, where visitors can enjoy matcha and wagashi.

Wagashi traces its history back to the Nara period (710–784), where its earliest incarnation took the form of humble treats such as dango and mochi. It was not until the Edo period (1603–1868), when the Japanese mastered the art of processing sugar from Okinawan sugarcane to create wasanbon – a sugar used exclusively to make wagashi – that Japan's traditional confectionery came to be. It was also during this time that wagashi was incorporated into chadō, the Japanese tea ceremony. Kyoto's skilled artisans, inspired by nature and the seasons, created wagashi in different delicate hues and shapes: craftsmanship that has been passed down through the centuries.

Types of wagashi

Wagashi falls into three different categories:

- namagashi (fresh wagashi)
- han namagashi (half-dry wagashi)
- higashi (dry wagashi)

It is further divided into different forms:

- mushi (steamed)
- yaki (baked)
- nagashi (jellied)
- neri (kneaded)
- uchi (molded)
- oshi (pressed)

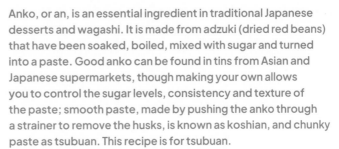

ANKO
RED BEAN PASTE

Anko, or an, is an essential ingredient in traditional Japanese desserts and wagashi. It is made from adzuki (dried red beans) that have been soaked, boiled, mixed with sugar and turned into a paste. Good anko can be found in tins from Asian and Japanese supermarkets, though making your own allows you to control the sugar levels, consistency and texture of the paste; smooth paste, made by pushing the anko through a strainer to remove the husks, is known as koshian, and chunky paste as tsubuan. This recipe is for tsubuan.

Anko only keeps for 5 days, but it can be used in the refreshing summer jelly known as Yōkan (below) and baked or steamed Black sugar buns (page 144).

MAKES 250 G (9 OZ)

150 g (5½ oz) adzuki (dried red beans)
100 g (3½ oz) caster (superfine) sugar

1   The day before you plan on using the anko, place the adzuki in a large bowl or container, cover with water by 2 cm (¾ in) and leave to soak overnight.

2   Drain the beans in a colander and rinse with running water, then transfer to a large saucepan along with 1 litre (1 qt) of water. Bring to the boil over medium heat, then reduce the heat to low and simmer for 20 minutes. Drain.

3   In a clean saucepan over low heat, bring 1 litre (1 qt) of water to a simmer, then add the sugar. Add the drained beans to the saucepan and simmer for 45–60 minutes, or until the beans come apart easily when squeezed. Remove from the heat, allow to cool and store in an airtight container in the fridge until needed.

YŌKAN
RED BEAN JELLY

MAKES APPROXIMATELY 24 PIECES

neutral oil, for greasing
1 quantity cooled Red bean paste (above)
8 g (¼ oz) agar-agar

1   Grease a 21 cm (8¼ in) square baking tin with oil. Strain the liquid from the anko into a bowl and reserve. Weigh the red beans from the red bean paste and add enough of the reserved liquid to make 1 kg (2 lb 3 oz). Discard the excess liquid.

2   Place the anko mixture in a saucepan. While the mixture is still cold, add the agar-agar and stir to combine.

3   Bring the anko mixture to a simmer over low heat, stirring constantly until the agar-agar completely dissolves. Pour into the prepared tin and set aside to cool to room temperature. Once it reaches room temperature, it should be set. Cover with plastic wrap and refrigerate overnight.

4   Cut the yōkan into small squares and serve.

KURO SATŌ MANJŪ

BLACK SUGAR BUNS

Originally from China, manjū were first brought to Japan in 1341, the most traditional filling being anko (red bean paste) encased within the cake-like 'buns'. Manjū can be baked or steamed (a common feature in onsen towns) and, being quite sweet, are best enjoyed with a cup of hot ocha (tea).

There is a plethora of manjū in Japan, differing from region to region and town to town. This particular recipe was inspired by manjū we had at a historic wagashi (Japanese sweet) shop in Nikko – two hours from Tokyo.

MAKES 20 BUNS

1 quantity Red bean
  paste (page 143)
100 g (3½ oz) black
  or brown sugar
50 g (1¾ oz) white
  (granulated) sugar
160 g (5¾ oz) plain
  (all-purpose) flour
40 g (1½ oz) potato starch
4 g (⅛ oz) baking soda
1 egg
1 tablespoon milk

1   Place the red bean paste in a large saucepan and bring to the boil over medium heat. Simmer until the mixture is thick enough that a line drawn through the mixture using a wooden spoon remains. Remove from the heat and allow to cool.

2   Scoop out 20 evenly sized portions of the cooled red bean paste and roll them into balls, then set aside.

3   In a small, clean saucepan, combine the black sugar, white sugar and 50 ml (1¾ fl oz) of water. Bring to a simmer over low heat and cook until the sugars dissolve. Remove from the heat and cool to room temperature, then add the flour, potato starch and baking soda and knead into a smooth and pliable dough.

4   Preheat the oven to 180°C (350°F) and line a baking tray with baking paper.

5   Divide the dough into 20 pieces. Flatten each piece into a disc, then place a ball of red bean paste in the centre of each. Wrap the dough around the red bean paste, pinching it together to seal, and shape it into a smooth oblong bun. Place each bun on the baking tray, seam-side down.

6   In a small bowl, beat the egg and milk together to make a wash and brush it over the buns.

7   Place the buns in the oven and reduce the heat to 130°C (270°F), then bake for 15 minutes. Cool on a wire rack and serve.

→
Clockwise from top left: Kuro Satō Manjū, Yōkan (page 143) and Anko (page 143)

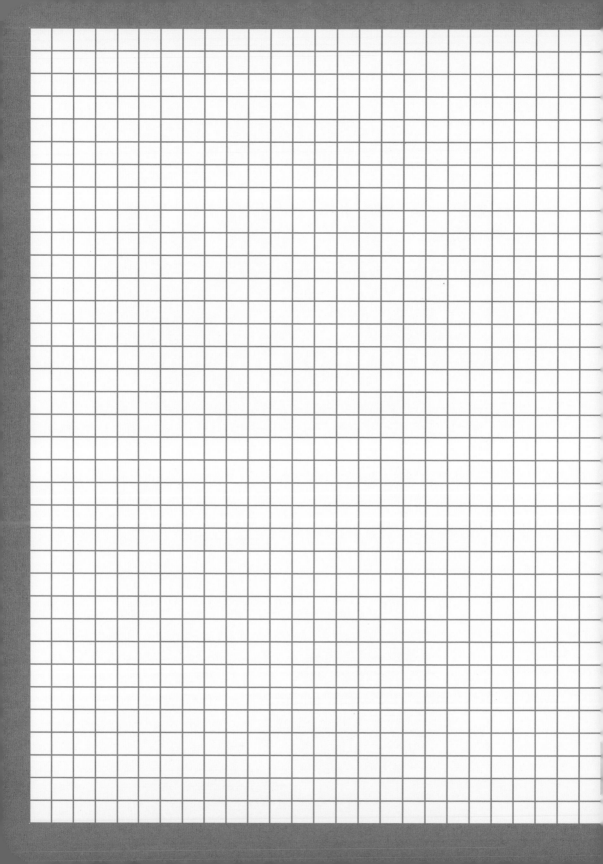

LATE

As the sun sets behind Mt Fuji, the neon lights of Tokyo flicker to life: the image of the city emblazoned in so many minds. Izakayas, restaurants and bars fill; beer, umeshu, highballs, chūhai and sake are raised to cheers of 'kanpai!', and the scent and sounds of nightlife in Japan fill the air.

Tokyo's night scene – outside of the reserved, hallowed dining establishments of kaiseki and kappo cuisine and Michelin-starred sushi-ya (sushi restaurants) – is fun, boisterous and lively. This is where locals shake off a long day, often staying out late into the night, catching the last trains out of the city.

Japanese establishments tend to focus on one cuisine, a reflection of their shokunin philosophy: the mastery of one craft by perfecting it over and over again. By contrast, the variety offered by izakaya – a smorgasbord of Japan's many cuisines – is what makes them so enticing. The paper menus plastering the walls cover everything from sake and beer snacks (burdock chips and grilled ginkgo nuts) to sashimi, monkfish liver with ponzu, sake- or saikyo miso–grilled fish, karaage (fried chicken), yakitori, gyūsuji nikomi (beef tendon stew) and motsunabe (offal stew). Start with a beverage and go from there.

Or perhaps wander down Shinjuku's Omoide Yokocho (Memory Lane) – an alleyway lined with tiny, crowded yakitori stalls that hark back to the late 1940s. Here, the smoke rises and billows as chefs stand over bubbling pots of tare (soy glaze, some of which have been carefully cultivated for decades) and charcoal grills, keeping a watchful eye

over skewers of chicken and motsu (offal). Skewers are ordered over the course of the evening (all at once is a rookie move, as you can't enjoy every skewer piping hot), called out to the chefs, who somehow manage to keep track. From here, it is a short walk to Golden Gai, Shinjuku's (in)famous warren of bars, for a drink.

Then there are the tachigui, or 'stand bars', which trace their origins back to food carts in 1600s Japan. Here you will find diners standing around long counters or tables, eating the tachigui's specialty – perhaps sushi, kaitenzushi (sushi train), steak or yakiniku (barbecued meat). Once – and still – a train-station staple (down a soba or udon before catching the next train), Tokyo's modern tachigui now feature premium cuts of beef from famous Japanese breeds, fish sourced that morning from Toyosu, and good wine and sake alongside Spanish–Japanese dishes.

Most nights end there, with salarymen bowing their goodbyes to colleagues at the train station. The bulk of the drinking, after all, is done over dinner. But some might continue on to a bar – often tucked away in a basement or at the top of a nondescript building – to enjoy a libation or two with jamon or namachoco (fresh chocolate).

RAMEN

This Tokyo-style shōyu (soy-based) ramen recipe calls for its various components to be made from scratch, so is best attempted over a weekend as a ramen project.

The great thing about this recipe is that the individual components can also be enjoyed separately: the chāshū (braised pork) is brilliant with takana (spicy mustard greens) and rice, and the ajitama (soy-seasoned egg) can be eaten on its own, with rice or a variety of Japanese dishes.

Aside from the ajitama, which keeps for three days, all other components can be kept in the fridge for up to five days, or used in Chilled ramen (page 155) or Abura soba (page 156).

Finally, dried and frozen ramen noodles can be found in Asian and Japanese supermarkets.

SERVES 4

finely sliced spring onions (scallions), to serve

Marinated bamboo shoots (page 156), to serve (optional)

nori, to serve

Chāshū (braised pork)

1 kg (2 lb 3 oz) rolled boneless, skinless pork belly

1 tablespoon salt

1 teaspoon sanshō (Japanese pepper)

1 litre (1 qt) soy sauce

300 g (10½ oz) caster (superfine) sugar

200 ml (6¾ fl oz) sake

1 tablespoon neutral oil, for frying

½ garlic clove

1 dried chilli

1 spring onion, green part only

Ajitama (soy-seasoned eggs)

4 eggs

400 ml (13½ fl oz) reserved Chāshū cooking liquid

1   The day before you plan to make ramen, prepare the chāshū for roasting. Season the pork with the salt and sanshō and place in the fridge, uncovered, to cure overnight.

2   The next day, place the soy sauce, sugar and sake in a saucepan over medium heat and cook until the sugar is dissolved. Set aside to cool.

3   Heat the oil in a large frying pan over very high heat until it begins to shimmer. Carefully sear the pork belly on all sides until browned. Transfer the pork to a large, heavy-based saucepan and add the cooled soy sauce mixture, garlic, chilli and spring onion, along with enough water to cover the pork.

4   Bring to the boil over medium heat, skimming away any impurities that rise to the surface. Cut out a circle of baking paper the same size as the mouth of the saucepan and place on top of the liquid; this will prevent it from evaporating too quickly. Reduce the heat to low and simmer for 2 hours.

5   Test that the pork belly is cooked by piercing it with a knife; it should go through easily. Carefully remove the pork belly from the cooking liquid and place on a wire rack. Refrigerate the pork until required (chilling the pork belly makes it easier to cut).

6   Strain and reserve the cooking liquid for the ajitama. You can also use the cooking liquid to make marinated bamboo shoots (page 156).

7   To make the ajitama, fill a large bowl with iced water. Bring a large saucepan of water to the boil over high heat.

Ramen broth

1 kg (2 lb 3 oz) chicken bones

500 g (1 lb 2 oz) pork bones

1 onion

1 apple, halved

1 carrot

2 spring onions, green part only

1 × 3 cm (1¼ in) piece ginger

1 × 4 cm (1½ in) piece konbu (dried kelp)

3 whole dried shiitake mushrooms

Ramen noodles

12 g (⅜ oz) kansui powder (potassium carbonate; see glossary), or 20 g (¾ oz) baking soda

600 g (1 lb 5 oz) plain (all-purpose) flour, or a combination of flours, such as 90% plain, 10% wholemeal (whole-wheat)

1 teaspoon salt

potato starch, to dust

Tare

100 g (3½ oz) chicken bones

250 ml (1 cup) soy sauce

1 tablespoon sake

1 whole dried shiitake mushroom

Flavoured oil (optional)

reserved fat from tare and ramen broth

1 tablespoon katsuobushi (dried skipjack tuna flakes)

8 Prick the bottom of the eggs with a thumb tack or special egg pricker (these can be found at Daiso, Tokyu Hands and Japanese ¥100 shops). This prevents the egg from splitting during boiling and creates an almost perfect oval shape.

9 Carefully place the eggs in the boiling water and boil for exactly 6 minutes, then transfer to the iced water using a slotted spoon. Set aside for 20 minutes to allow them to cool completely. After 20 minutes, peel the eggs and immerse them in the reserved chāshū cooking liquid. Transfer them to the fridge to marinate for 6–8 hours.

10 To make the ramen broth, place the chicken and pork bones in a large stockpot, along with 1.5 litres (1½ qts) of water. Bring to the boil over medium heat, then reduce the heat to low and simmer for 2 hours, regularly skimming away any impurities that rise to the surface, until the foam turns white.

11 Add the onion, apple, carrot, spring onions and ginger and cook for 30 minutes. Add the konbu and mushrooms and simmer for 1 hour.

12 Strain the broth into a container, discarding the solids, and chill in the fridge. After chilling, scrape off the solidified fat that has risen to the surface and reserve for the flavoured oil, if making.

13 To make the noodles, you first need to prepare the alkaline solution that gives the noodles their springy texture and yellow colour.

14 If you are using baking soda, preheat the oven to 200°C (400°F) and line a tray with baking paper. Spread the baking soda onto the tray and bake for 1 hour, stirring every 15 minutes. This converts the baking soda into sodium carbonate, an alkaline powder like kansui powder.

15 Whisk the kansui powder or sodium carbonate with 300 ml (10¼ fl oz) of water; this is your alkaline solution.

16 Place the flour and salt in a large mixing bowl and slowly trickle in the alkaline solution. Mix by hand until it forms a very stiff dough, adding more water if it is too tough to knead. The dough should be hard but malleable, and shouldn't crumble.

17 Roll the dough out into a rectangle as best as you can and feed it through the widest setting of a pasta machine.

Continues next page →

Fold the dough in half and feed it through the machine once more. Reduce the width between the rollers and feed the dough through again. Continue this process until the dough is approximately 3–4 mm (⅛ in) thick.

18   Using a sharp knife or the pasta cutter on the pasta machine, slice the dough into thin noodles and dust liberally with potato starch to prevent them from sticking. Cover with plastic wrap and transfer to the fridge until you are ready to cook the noodles.

19   To make the tare, preheat the oven to 180°C (350°F). Place the chicken bones in a roasting tin and roast for 45 minutes. If making the flavoured oil, strain the juices that have collected in the bottom of the tin and set aside with the ramen broth fat. Transfer the roasted bones to a large saucepan over medium heat and add the remaining ingredients. Bring to the boil, then reduce the heat to low and simmer for 45 minutes. Transfer to the fridge to chill, then strain into a bowl and set aside.

20   If making the flavoured oil, place the reserved fats and katsuobushi in a small saucepan and bring to a simmer over low heat. Cook for 5 minutes, then remove from the heat. When cool, strain the oil into a bowl and discard the katsuobushi.

21   To assemble one bowl of ramen (simply multiply the quantities below if serving more than one; this recipe makes enough for four bowls), bring 300 ml (10¼ fl oz) of the ramen broth to the boil in a saucepan over medium heat.

22   Slice the chāshū into 5 mm (¼ in) slices.

23   Fill a separate large saucepan with water and bring to the boil over high heat. Measure out 150 g (5½ oz) of the ramen noodles and place in the boiling water. Cook for 3 minutes (or follow the packet instructions if you are using store-bought noodles).

24   Meanwhile, place 1 tablespoon of the tare and ½ teaspoon of the flavoured oil (if using) in a warm bowl and add the hot ramen broth. Drain the cooked noodles well and add to the bowl, mixing to incorporate the tare and oil. Top with two pieces of the chāshū, one ramen egg, 1 tablespoon of the spring onion, 1 tablespoon of the marinated bamboo shoots (if using) and one sheet of nori. Serve immediately.

Note
This noodle recipe produces a thicker, Tokyo-style noodle with a chewy texture like that of mochi. Increasing the water content results in a more mochi-like texture, while reducing the water content results in a more wiry or 'snappy' texture that is common in Hakata-style tonkotsu ramen. It is very difficult to produce a very low water content noodle without the use of a ramen machine.

HIYASHI CHŪKA

CHILLED RAMEN

Tokyo summers are hot and humid, and you can't help but crave cool things like watermelon, sofuto kurimu (soft-serve ice cream), kakigori (shaved ice) and chilled noodle dishes like Zaru soba (page 96) and zaru udon.

Hiyashi chūka is said to have been invented by a Chinese restaurant in Sendai in 1937. It is a dish that signifies summer, with ramen-ya (noodle shops) and Chinese restaurants putting out signs that read 'Hiyashi chūka hajimemashita', or 'We've started serving hiyashi chūka', once the temperature starts to rise.

Hiyashi chūkamen, to use its full name, means 'chilled Chinese-style noodles' and is a cold ramen, served with ribbons of ham, cucumber, omelette, tomato and seaweed as toppings, along with a refreshingly salty and citrusy dressing. It's an incredibly effortless dish to make. There is little cooking involved besides blanching the ramen and frying the egg – perfect in the summer heat!

SERVES 1

1 egg, beaten

½ tomato

150 g (5½ oz) fresh Ramen noodles (page 151)

25 g (1 oz) ham, julienned

½ cucumber, julienned

¼ daikon (Japanese radish), julienned

1 tablespoon kizami nori (finely shredded nori; see glossary)

1 tablespoon wakame (sea mustard; see glossary), rehydrated if dried

1 lemon wedge

Sauce

120 ml (4 fl oz) Ponzu (page 225)

120 ml (4 fl oz) black vinegar

2 teaspoons caster (superfine) sugar

1 teaspoon sesame oil

1   To make the sauce, whisk all of the ingredients in a bowl until the sugar dissolves. Cover and transfer to the fridge to chill. This recipe makes 250 ml (1 cup) of sauce, enough for four serves.

2   Heat a non-stick frying pan over medium heat. Pour in the beaten egg, tilting the pan to spread the egg and create a thin omelette. When the omelette is cooked through, remove from the pan, shred and set aside.

3   Using a sharp knife, score a cross into the skin of the tomato. Fill a large bowl with iced water. Bring a large saucepan of water to the boil over high heat. Blanch the tomato in the boiling water for 10 seconds, then transfer to the iced water using a slotted spoon. Peel the tomato by pulling the skin away from the cross. Finely slice the flesh of the tomato, discarding the seeds, and set aside.

4   Blanch the ramen noodles in the boiling water for 1½ minutes, or until cooked, then drain and transfer immediately to the iced water. Once the noodles are cool, drain them well.

5   To serve, place the noodles in a bowl. Arrange the ham, vegetables, kizami nori, wakame and shredded omelette on top, then dress with 60 ml (¼ cup) of the sauce. Mix everything together before eating, accompanied by a squeeze of fresh lemon.

ABURA SOBA

Abura soba, contrary to its name, is not actually soba, or buckwheat noodles, but a dry-style ramen created in Tokyo's Kitatama district in the 1950s. The abura – oil – comes from the rendered pork fat layered over a soy sauce blend called tare. Fresh ramen noodles are added to the bowl, followed by toppings, including marinated bamboo shoots, spring onions (scallions), nori and chāshū (braised pork).

Just before eating, the noodles are mixed together, the flavoured oil giving them a lovely sheen. It's a wonderfully satisfying, addictive dish, and if you fancy, you can also add extra condiments, such as onion, chilli paste, sanshō (Japanese pepper), chilli oil and vinegar.

Fresh bamboo shoots are hard to come by outside Japan, and while it is easy to find tinned varieties, they often have a particular taste. This recipe removes the tinned flavour and infuses the bamboo shoots with a delicious chāshū and bonito marinade.

SERVES 1

150 g (5½ oz) fresh Ramen noodles (page 151)

2 tablespoons Tare (page 151)

1 tablespoon Flavoured oil (page 151)

1 piece Braised pork (page 150)

1 tablespoon kizami nori (finely shredded nori; see glossary)

1 tablespoon finely sliced spring onion (scallion)

½ onion, finely diced

rice vinegar and chilli oil, to serve

Menma (marinated bamboo shoots)

1 × 400 g (14 oz) tin sliced bamboo shoots, drained

200 ml (6¾ fl oz) reserved Braised pork cooking liquid (see page 150)

1 handful of hanakatsuo (dried skipjack tuna flakes)

1   First, make the menma. Place the bamboo shoots in a saucepan and cover with water, then bring to the boil over high heat and boil for 5 minutes. Drain and repeat the process two more times. This removes the tinned taste from the bamboo shoots and makes it easier for the marinade to be absorbed.

2   Return the drained bamboo shoots to the saucepan and add the braised pork cooking liquid and enough water to cover. Bring to a simmer over medium heat.

3   Place a sheet of paper towel on top of the liquid, followed by the hanakatsuo. Simmer for 5 minutes, then remove from the heat and allow to cool to room temperature. Discard the paper towel and hanakatsuo. Reserve 1 tablespoon of bamboo shoots for this recipe and transfer the remaining bamboo shoots and liquid to an airtight container. The menma will keep in the fridge for up to 4 days.

4   Bring a large saucepan of water to the boil over high heat. Cook the ramen noodles for 3 minutes (or follow the packet instructions if you are using store-bought noodles) and drain thoroughly.

5   To assemble the abura soba, place the tare and flavoured oil in the bottom of a warm serving bowl, followed by the noodles. Top with the braised pork, menma, kizami nori and spring onion.

6   Mix together just before eating. Add diced onion, rice vinegar and chilli oil to taste.

YAKITORI

Yakitori is a pretty recent dish in Japan's culinary history, soaring in popularity only after World War II. This was partly because chicken was considered a luxury in ancient Japan, with the earliest yakitori stalls of the Edo period (1603–1868) serving the off-cuts (usually offal and gristle) from high-end chicken restaurants.

Today, salarymen crowd around the smoky counters of yatai (street carts) and yakitori-ya (yakitori shops), beer in hand, calling out their orders. There are also more upscale yakitori establishments that showcase chicken breeds from different prefectures, cooked over special binchotan (charcoal), with different cuts prepared using different methods. You might find chicken sashimi and a clear, rich chicken broth on the menu, and toppings on the counter such as wasabi, Yuzukoshō (page 226), Shichimi tōgarashi (page 227) and sanshō (Japanese pepper).

It is hard to beat the irresistible scent and flavour of yakitori grilled over binchotan, but if you don't have a charcoal grill at home, you can use a regular grill (broiler) or pan-fry the chicken. The two recipes here feature the chicken glazed in a glorious soy-based sauce (tare), but in Japan, you have the option of having it 'shio' – simply sprinkled with salt. The tsukune (chicken meatballs) are usually eaten dipped in raw egg, but using Hot-spring eggs (page 219) is just as delicious.

Yakitori tare

150 ml (5 fl oz) soy sauce
150 ml (5 fl oz) mirin
50 ml (1¾ fl oz) sake
100 g (3½ oz) raw sugar
2 spring onion (scallion) tops

Negima (spring onion and chicken thigh)

500 g (1 lb 2 oz) skinless,
    boneless chicken thighs
2 bunches spring onions,
    white and light green parts
    only, cut into 2.5 cm (1 in)
    lengths

Tsukune (chicken meatballs)

½ onion, finely chopped
500 g (1 lb 2 oz) minced
    (ground) chicken (see note)
50 g (1¾ oz) chicken cartilage,
    finely chopped (optional)
1 egg white
50 g (1¾ oz) silken tofu
1 tablespoon salt
1 teaspoon freshly ground
    black pepper
1 tablespoon cornflour
    (corn starch)
panko breadcrumbs,
    for thickening (optional)

1   First, make the yakitori tare. Place all of the ingredients, except the spring onion tops, in a saucepan over medium heat and cook until reduced by one-quarter. Add the spring onion tops and simmer for another 10 minutes, then strain into a bowl. The tare can be cooled and stored in an airtight container in the fridge for up to 1 month.

2   If using bamboo skewers, soak them in water so they do not burn during cooking.

3   To make the negima, cut each thigh into four pieces and thread onto skewers, alternating between the meat and the spring onion. Season with salt and cover and place in the fridge until you are ready to cook.

4   To make the tsukune, soak the chopped onion in water for 15 minutes. Meanwhile, mix the chicken mince and cartilage (if using) with the egg white, tofu, salt and pepper, until everything is well incorporated. Drain the onion and pat dry with paper towel, combine with the cornflour, then add to the chicken mixture. If the mixture is too soft to work with, add 1 tablespoon of panko and incorporate, repeating the process if necessary until the mixture is firm enough to be shaped.

5   Shape the mixture into balls about the size of ping-pong balls, and thread two onto each skewer. Cover and place in the fridge until you are ready to cook.

6   Grill the skewers over charcoal. Just before the negima are completely cooked through, brush with the tare and continue cooking until done. If you are unsure whether or not they are fully cooked, you can cut the centre piece with a knife to see if the inside is opaque and cooked.

7   Dip both the tsukune and the negima in the tare and serve.

8   Alternatively, if you do not have a charcoal grill, pan-fry the negima and brush with tare as above.

9   Bake the tsukune in a 180°C (350°F) oven for 8 minutes, then pan-fry until browned on the outside. Dip both the tsukune and the negima in the tare and serve.

Note
For richer, gamier tsukune, substitute the chicken mince for duck mince.

OKONOMIYAKI

Okonomiyaki is a Japanese-style grilled pancake filled with cabbage, seafood, egg and meat. A portmanteau of 'what you want' and 'grilled' in Japanese. Monjayaki is Tokyo's take on the classic.

It is dusk. The bustle of nearby Sensōji , Asakusa's famous temple with its towering red and black lantern, has died down, the lingering scent of ningyoyaki (sweet cakes filled with adzuki bean paste) and senbei (rice crackers) fading into the night air. We're walking down the side streets of the old neighbourhood, trying to track down a place called Sometarō, Japan's first monjayaki restaurant, which has been around since 1937.

Okonomiyaki's claim to fame lies in Osaka, where it was created in 1930, and Hiroshima, which has a different style entirely. Natives of Osaka also pronounce their city to be the place where someone first added mayonnaise as an okonomiyaki topping. Okonomiyaki isn't really Tokyo's calling, but we are tracking down this shop because unlike its southern brethren, you don't watch someone cook the dish: you cook the monjayaki.

But we are hopelessly lost, until an elderly granny totters up to us, looks at our map and beckons us to follow her. We insist that with directions we can locate it ourselves. But this is Japan, and the granny will have none of that.

She will take us there, she says, and leads us right to the doorstep of a Shōwa-era (1926–1989) Japanese shophouse. Much bowing and profuse thanking ensues, before we step past the noren into the shop, simply furnished with tatami mats and zabuton laid around low grills, where we will cook the monjayaki.

This is food made for nama bīru (draught beer) and friendships. As the light fades, groups pile in: salarymen, girls catching up, and older grandpas who live locally. The proprietress bustles around, handing out small cubes of lard, bowls filled with batter, plates of ingredients (seafood, the ubiquitous cabbage, egg, meat), and for the uninitiated, a sheet of pictorial instructions carefully encased in plastic.

Here, Tokyoites lose their inhibitions. Laughter and giggles fill the air as diners show off their cooking prowess, whipping the batter, frying the monjayaki, slathering on Bull-Dog sauce and Kewpie mayo, and dusting their results with seaweed flakes. And as the night deepens, the chatter rises, the batter sizzles, and diners call out, 'Okawari!' (refill).

The other styles of Okonomiyaki

Osaka-style (also known as Kansai-style)

Osaka's okonomiyaki are denser than their Tokyo counterparts, and filled with ingredients such as yamaimo (a sticky local yam), cabbage, spring onions (scallions) , pork, bacon, squid, prawns (shrimp), octopus, mochi, kimchi and cheese. Mixed into a batter and then grilled on both sides over a teppan (hot plate), the okonomiyaki is finished with Worcestershire-based sauce (Bull-Dog being the favoured brand), Kewpie mayonnaise, katsuobushi (dried skipjack tuna flakes), aonori (powdered seaweed flakes), spring onions and beni shōga (pickled ginger).

Hiroshima-style

Hiroshima's okonomiyaki feature noodles (yakisoba or udon), a fried egg and copious amounts of shredded cabbage. Unlike Osaka, the okonomiyaki is built in layers, with a thin, crepe-like layer of batter at the bottom laying the foundation for a pile of cabbage, upon which the other ingredients are balanced. It is then flipped onto a pile of noodles and topped with lashings of okonomiyaki sauce and a fried egg.

Hashimaki-style

'Hashi' means chopsticks, and hashimaki is okonomiyaki on a stick. An invention from the Kansai region (that's Osaka again), hashimaki can be found at matsuri (festivals) throughout Japan, and is a popular street-stall snack.

MONJAYAKI

TOKYO-STYLE
OKONOMIYAKI

Monjayaki is okonomiyaki's cousin, and unlike its aesthetically pleasing relatives from Osaka and Hiroshima, it is less like a pancake and more like a hot batter that serves as a sauce for the ingredients. But while it may not be attractive, it is no less delicious, and making it is a fun way to spend an evening with friends, especially if you have a portable stove and hot plate that can be set up in the middle of the dining table.

The ingredients are an entirely personal choice, and may include traditional options like meat, cuttlefish, scallops, oysters and prawns (shrimp), or more unorthodox inclusions, such as mentaiko (spicy pollock roe), cheese, mochi and corn.

Tsukishima in Tokyo has a monjayaki strip, filled with more than a hundred restaurants selling the dish. Beer is a recommended accompaniment.

SERVES 2

350 ml (11¾ fl oz) Konbu dashi (page 221)

35 g (¼ cup) plain (all-purpose) flour

2 tablespoons oyster sauce

1 tablespoon oil, for frying

300 g (10½ oz) cabbage, shredded

2 tablespoons dried prawns (shrimp)

your choice of meat, vegetables and seafood, such as bacon, bean sprouts, prawns or squid

aonori (powdered seaweed flakes; see glossary), to serve

tenkasu (see note on page 107), to serve

mayonnaise (preferably Kewpie), to serve (optional)

1   To make the monjayaki batter, combine the konbu dashi, flour and oyster sauce in a bowl.

2   Place a portable stove in the centre of your table and use it to heat the oil on a hotplate over medium heat. Add the cabbage, dried prawns, and meat, vegetables and seafood of choice, and fry until cooked through, using spatulas or spoons to break up the ingredients into bite-sized pieces.

3   Gather the ingredients into the middle of the hotplate, then create a well in the centre. Pour the batter into the well and cook, stirring constantly and incorporating the ingredients on the hotplate, until it thickens.

4   To serve, top the monjayaki with aonori and tenkasu, and drizzle with a little mayonnaise (if using).

CHAWANMUSHI

SAVOURY EGG CUSTARD

Created in Nagasaki in the 18th century, chawanmushi is a steamed savoury egg custard with a silken texture and a delicate umami flavour. Part of the pleasure of eating chawanmushi is finding the ingredients buried within, which can range from kamaboko (a pink and white fishcake) and prawn (shrimp), to chicken, shiitake mushrooms, ginkgo nut and mochi. The most luxurious chawanmushi often include uni (sea urchin) and ikura (salmon roe) on top, with crabmeat and gold leaf.

SERVES 4 AS A STARTER

a selection of meat and vegetables such as prawn (shrimp), chicken, ginkgo nut and okra

2 eggs

250 ml (1 cup) Katsuo dashi (page 220)

1 tablespoon soy sauce

1 tablespoon mirin

1 tablespoon sake

Gin-an sauce (page 223), to serve

grated ginger, to serve

1 Fill a large saucepan with water. Place a large bamboo steamer on top of the saucepan and bring to the boil over medium heat.

2 Divide the selection of meat and vegetables between four ramekins or small serving bowls. Blend together the eggs, katsuo dashi, soy sauce, mirin and sake until well combined. Skim any bubbles off the top of the egg mixture, then divide it between the four ramekins and cover each one with plastic wrap.

3 Place the ramekins in the steamer and increase the heat to high. Steam for 10–12 minutes, or until a skewer inserted into the centre of a chawanmushi comes out clean.

4 Cover each chawanmushi with gin-an sauce and dot with grated ginger. Serve hot.

KANIKOROKKE

CRAB CROQUETTES

Japan's korokke are inspired by the French croquette, which was introduced to the country in 1887. There are two types: a potato-based version usually made with minced (ground) beef and onions, and a cream-based one made with crab or prawn (shrimp).

Korokke can be found at street stalls, handed to you in a paper wrapper, crisp and piping hot. It's a treat in the cold weather, when customers huddle on the footpath around the stall, huffing and puffing on the korokke to cool it down while they savour their creamy (or carb-y) warmth.

While best eaten hot, korokke can also be served in bentō or wedged between bread to make a sandwich or burger (see our Katsu burger recipe, page 118). The crab in this recipe can be substituted with prawn.

SERVES 4

95 g (3¼ oz) unsalted butter

245g (8¾ oz) plain (all-purpose) flour, divided into 95g (3¼ oz) and 150g (5½ oz)

300 ml (10¼ fl oz) milk, plus 1 tablespoon

1 tablespoon olive oil

1 onion, finely diced

50 ml (1¾ fl oz) white wine or sake

100 g (3½ oz) cooked crabmeat

40 ml (1¼ fl oz) thin (pouring) cream

3 eggs

1 tablespoon chopped parsley, plus extra to serve

60 g (1 cup) panko breadcrumbs

neutral oil, for deep-frying

Tomato sauce

1 tomato

1 tablespoon olive oil

1 carrot, chopped

1 onion, chopped

1 celery stalk, chopped

1 garlic clove, chopped

1 tablespoon tomato paste (concentrated puree)

100 ml (3½ fl oz) white wine or sake

250 ml (1 cup) chicken stock or water

Tabasco sauce, to taste

1   First, make the tomato sauce. Using a sharp knife, score a cross in the base of the tomato and remove the core. Fill a large bowl with iced water. Blanch the tomato in boiling water for 10 seconds, then transfer to the iced water using a slotted spoon. Peel the tomato by pulling the skin away from the cross. Chop the remaining flesh.

2   Heat the olive oil in a saucepan over medium heat and fry the carrot, onion, celery and garlic until soft. Add the tomato paste and fry until the paste darkens and caramelises. Pour in the wine and reduce the liquid by half, scraping up any bits stuck to the pan. Finally, add the chopped tomato and chicken stock.

3   Bring the sauce to the boil, reduce the heat to low and simmer for 5 minutes. Remove from the heat to cool slightly, then blend until smooth. Season with salt, pepper and Tabasco to taste.

4   To make the korokke, melt the butter in a saucepan over medium–low heat. Add 95 g (3¼ oz) of the flour and cook, stirring constantly, for about 3 minutes, until the colour just begins to change.

5   Add the milk in four batches, stirring to incorporate well after each addition. Season with salt, transfer to a large mixing bowl and set aside to cool.

6   In a separate saucepan, heat the olive oil over medium heat and cook the onion until soft. Add the wine and cook until the mixture is reduced to a syrup. Remove from the heat and set aside to cool to room temperature.

7   When cool, add the wine reduction, crabmeat, cream, an egg and the chopped parsley to the flour mixture and stir to combine well. Line a baking tray with baking paper and shape the mixture into 20 ovals, placing each one on the prepared tray. Cover with plastic wrap, then refrigerate to set the shape, about 1 hour.

8   In a large, shallow bowl, whisk the remaining eggs together until homogenous. Spread the remaining flour on a large plate and the panko on a separate plate. Take one oval and dredge it in the flour. Brush off any excess and dip the oval in the beaten egg, followed by the panko, making sure it is well coated in breadcrumbs. Repeat with the remaining ovals.

9   Fill a large, heavy-based saucepan one-third of the way with oil. Heat over medium heat to 180°C (350°F) – a pinch of flour dropped into the oil should sizzle on contact – and deep-fry the korokke for 3–5 minutes, until golden. Sprinkle with parsley and serve with the tomato sauce.

EBI TO YASAI NO SU ZERĪ

PRAWNS AND VEGETABLES WITH VINEGAR JELLY

This refreshing dish is often served in summer as part of kappō or kaiseki cuisine, and makes for a pretty starter. Chilled prawns (shrimp) are topped with star-shaped okra, translucent umi budo (sea grapes), delicate little purple shiso (perilla) flowers and gold-hued vinegar jelly.

The flavours are a wonderful combination too, with tartness from the jelly and tomato, and saltiness from the prawn and sea grapes, which burst in the mouth to release the taste of the ocean. Deceptively simple, the dish only requires a little advance preparation to set the jelly.

SERVES 4

1 tomato

2 tablespoons salt

4 okra pods

4 asparagus spears

8 whole raw prawns (shrimp)

4 shiso (perilla) leaves, shredded, to garnish

shiso buds, to garnish (optional)

4 umi budo (sea grapes; see glossary), to garnish (optional)

Jelly

2 sheets gold-strength leaf gelatine

200 ml (6¾ fl oz) Katsuo dashi (page 220)

100 ml (3½ fl oz) rice vinegar

1 tablespoon soy sauce

1 tablespoon caster (superfine) sugar

1   To make the jelly, soak the gelatine leaves in cold water to soften. In a saucepan over medium heat, bring the remaining jelly ingredients to a simmer. When the sugar has dissolved completely, remove the mixture from the heat. Squeeze the water out of the gelatine leaves and add them to the saucepan, whisking until they dissolve. Pour the liquid into an airtight container and transfer to the fridge to set overnight.

2   Using a sharp knife, score a cross in the base of the tomato and remove the core. Fill a large bowl with iced water. Bring a large saucepan of water to the boil over high heat and add the salt. Blanch the okra in the boiling water for 1 minute, or until it turns bright green, then transfer to the iced water using a slotted spoon. Repeat the process with the asparagus and then the tomato, keeping the tomato in the boiling water for 10 seconds to loosen the skin.

3   Peel the tomato by pulling the skin away from the cross and cut it into quarters, discarding the seeds. Cut each asparagus spear into three pieces, then cut the okra into bite-sized pieces.

4   Reduce the heat so the salted water is at a simmer, then cook the prawns for 2–3 minutes before transferring to the iced water. Peel and devein the prawns.

5   To serve, arrange the prawns and vegetables on individual plates, then break up the jelly with a whisk and spoon over the top. Garnish with the shiso leaves and buds and umi budo.

TAICHAZUKE

SNAPPER OCHAZUKE

Ochazuke – 'ocha' meaning tea and 'zuke' meaning to submerge – is a dish of rice with seasonal toppings and a fragrant, hot dashi or tea broth poured over the top. The toppings vary from region to region, from a simple ochazuke of pickles, umeboshi (pickled plum) and nori, to ochazuke with Salt-grilled salmon (page 28), kingfish and tuna sashimi, mentaiko (spicy pollock roe) and kakiage (vegetable and seafood fritters).

In this recipe, we use snapper cured with konbu (dried kelp) and sake, which firms up the flesh and brings out the fish's umami flavour.

SERVES 4

1 skinless sashimi-grade snapper fillet, deboned (see note)

1 × 20 cm (8 in) piece konbu (dried kelp), soaked in cold water for 15 minutes to rehydrate, or reserved from making dashi (see pages 220–221), cut in half widthways

1 tablespoon sake

1 tablespoon salt

rice, to serve

arare (puffed rice crisps; see glossary), to serve

kizami nori (finely shredded nori; see glossary), to serve

wasabi, to serve

Ichiban dashi

800 ml (27 fl oz) Katsuo dashi (page 220)

50 ml (1¾ fl oz) light soy sauce

50 ml (1¾ fl oz) sake

1   Thoroughly dry the snapper fillet and konbu with paper towels. Lay one piece of konbu on a large piece of plastic wrap and evenly sprinkle half of the sake and half of the salt on top.

2   Slice the snapper very thinly and arrange on top of the seasoned konbu. Sprinkle with the remaining sake and salt and cover with the other sheet of konbu. Wrap the snapper tightly in the plastic wrap and place in the fridge to cure for 15–30 minutes. The cured fish will be firmer and slightly salty.

3   Warm the katsuo dashi in a saucepan over low heat and add the soy sauce and sake, seasoning with salt to taste.

4   To serve, place a mound of rice in each bowl and top with the cured snapper, arare, kizami nori and a small amount of wasabi. Transfer the warmed dashi to a vessel with a spout, such as a pitcher or a teapot, and allow your diners to pour in as much or as little dashi as they like.

Note

Taichazuke is usually made with tai, or red sea bream (*Pagrus major*). This can be difficult to find in Australia, so we have substituted its close relative, Australasian snapper (*Pagrus auratus*). You may like to use another kind of sweet, firm-fleshed white fish in its place.

TAIMESHI
SNAPPER RICE

We were once seated – by pure chance – in the private dining room of a renowned Japanese kaiseki restaurant in Kyoto. The room was traditionally Japanese in style, with little by way of decoration. There was, however, one single piece of artwork on the wall: a picture of a whole tai, or red sea bream.

Tai is a symbolic food in Japanese culture, reserved for celebrations and important days such as the Japanese New Year. The word 'madai' – 'genuine tai' – sounds like the word for auspicious, 'medetai', thus the fish is believed to be a harbinger of good luck. Taimeshi, sea bream cooked with rice, is a specialty of Ehime Prefecture and a symbol of celebration. It's a delicious dish rich in umami, the blanching of the tai and the addition of ginger removing the fishy flavour.

SERVES 4

1 × 300 g (10½ oz) snapper, cleaned and scaled, or 2 × 100 g (3½ oz) snapper fillets

400 g (2 cups) Japanese short-grain rice

60 ml (¼ cup) light soy sauce

2 tablespoons sake

1 × 3 cm (1¼ in) piece ginger, peeled and shredded

1 × 5 cm (2 in) piece konbu (dried kelp)

4 shiso (perilla) leaves, shredded

Miso soup (page 29), to serve

Note
Red sea bream (*Pagrus major*) – can be difficult to find in Australia, so we have substituted its close relative, Australasian snapper (*Pagrus auratus*). You may like to use another kind of sweet, firm-fleshed white fish in its place.

1   Using a pair of kitchen shears, carefully (as the fins are sharp) cut off the tail fin, side fins and dorsal fin of the snapper.

2   Fill a large bowl with iced water. Bring a large saucepan of water to the boil over high heat and blanch the snapper for 1 minute. Drain the snapper, then transfer to the iced water to refresh. When cool, run your fingers carefully along the skin to remove any remaining scales. Drain again and and dry both the inside and outside of the fish thoroughly with paper towels.

3   To wash the rice, place in a sieve and submerge it in a large bowl filled with water. Using your palms, gently rub the rice back and forth in the sieve. When the water turns cloudy, drain the bowl, refill it with fresh water, and repeat the washing process another two times, or until the water runs clear. Drain the rice well.

4   Place the rice, 500 ml (2 cups) of water, the soy sauce and sake in a rice cooker or large saucepan with a lid and stir to combine. Taste and add salt if required. Scatter the ginger over the surface, add the konbu, then arrange the snapper on top.

5   Cook the rice on a rice cooker's normal rice setting until the cooking cycle is complete. If using a saucepan, bring to the boil over medium heat, then cover and reduce the heat to very low. Cook for 10 minutes, then remove from the heat and set aside to rest for 10–15 minutes, until the liquid has been fully absorbed.

6   Carefully debone the fish, then stir the rice to combine everything. Top with the shiso and serve with miso soup.

EBI DORIA
PRAWNS DORIA

Doria was invented by the same grand chef who brought Purin à la mode (page 136) to Japan: Swiss chef S. Weil of the Hotel New Grand in Yokohama. Created in 1927, the dish featured prawns (shrimp) and scallops simmered in a luxurious creamy sauce, which was draped over rice cooked in the finest butter. The doria was then topped with cheese and grilled (broiled) – a Japanese take on the French gratin.

Seafood doria is still served in the Hotel New Grand today, but this version is inspired by the one at the Hotel Okura. Plain rice can be used in lieu of the butter rice for a lighter version.

SERVES 4

1 tablespoon butter

½ onion, finely diced

100 g (3½ oz) button
mushrooms, stems removed

400 g (14 oz) raw prawns
(shrimp), peeled
and deveined

3 tablespoons white wine

neutral oil, for greasing

100 g (3½ oz) hard cheese,
such as gruyere, cheddar
or parmesan, shredded

1 handful of parsley,
finely chopped

green salad, to serve

Sauce

400 ml (13½ fl oz) milk

50 g (1¾ oz) butter

60 g (2 oz) plain (all-purpose)
flour

Butter rice

300 g (10½ oz) Japanese
short-grain rice

100 g (3½ oz) butter

½ onion, finely diced

1 teaspoon salt

½ teaspoon paprika

1 pinch of cayenne pepper

1 pinch of freshly ground
black pepper

1 bay leaf

1 Start by making the doria sauce. Warm the milk in a saucepan over low heat, taking care not to let it boil. In a separate saucepan over medium heat, melt the butter and add the flour. Stir constantly for 3 minutes, until the colour changes very slightly. Add the milk in three stages, stirring well to incorporate after each addition. Season with salt and pepper to taste and set aside.

2 Next make the butter rice. To wash the rice, place it in a sieve and submerge it in a large bowl filled with water. Using your palms, gently rub the rice back and forth in the sieve. When the water turns cloudy, drain the bowl, refill it with fresh water, and repeat the washing process another two times, or until the water runs clear. Drain the rice well.

3 Melt the butter in a large, heavy-based saucepan with a lid over medium heat and cook the onion until soft. Add the rice and stir for 1 minute to coat the rice grains in butter. Pour in 400 ml (13½ fl oz) of water and add the salt, paprika, cayenne pepper, black pepper and bay leaf.

4 Cover and bring to the boil, then reduce the heat to low and cook for 14 minutes. After 14 minutes, remove from the heat but keep covered and set aside to rest for 10 minutes.

5 Preheat the oven to 200°C (400°F).

6 In a large frying pan over medium–high heat, melt the butter and add the onion and button mushrooms. Fry until browned, then add the prawns. As soon as the colour of the prawns changes, add the white wine and stir through, then remove from the heat. Season with salt and pepper to taste.

7 To assemble the doria, grease a large baking dish or four individual dishes with oil. Spread the rice over the base of the dish, followed by the prawn and mushroom mix, the sauce and finally the cheese. Place the dish on a baking tray and bake in the oven for 10–15 minutes, or until golden brown. Remove from the oven, sprinkle with parsley and serve hot with a green salad.

BURI DAIKON

**BRAISED KINGFISH
AND DAIKON**

A warming fish stew, buri daikon is a home-cooked dish with a nostalgic flavour. It is typically found in Japan in winter, when the kingfish is fatty and rich in flavour, and daikon (Japanese radish) comes into season. The addition of ginger, along with the blanching process, removes the fishy scent and flavour from the kingfish.

SERVES 4

1 large daikon (Japanese radish), cut into 2 cm (¾ in) discs

1 handful of uncooked rice

4 × 150 g (5½ oz) kingfish fillets, deboned

1 litre (1 qt) Konbu dashi (page 221)

200 ml (6¾ fl oz) sake

1 × 4 cm (1½ in) piece ginger, shredded

3 tablespoons soy sauce

1 tablespoon caster (superfine) sugar

2 tablespoons mirin

1 teaspoon salt

1 handful of spinach leaves

rice, to serve

1   Place the daikon and uncooked rice in a large saucepan and cover with water. Bring to the boil over medium heat and cook for 20 minutes, or until a knife easily pierces all the way through the daikon. Drain the daikon and discard the liquid and rice. This step removes the bitterness from the daikon.

2   Fill a large bowl with iced water. Bring a saucepan of water to the boil over high heat and blanch the kingfish fillets in the boiling water until their colour changes. Drain the kingfish, then transfer to the iced water to refresh. Drain again and dry thoroughly with paper towels.

3   In a large saucepan over medium heat, bring the konbu dashi, sake and ginger to a simmer, then add the kingfish, daikon, soy sauce, sugar, mirin and salt. Cut out a circle of baking paper the same size as the mouth of the saucepan and place on top of the liquid; this will prevent it from evaporating too quickly. Reduce the heat to low and cook for 15 minutes.

4   Divide the daikon and kingfish among four bowls. Place the spinach in the hot cooking liquid until it is wilted, then add it to the bowls, pouring some liquid on top. Serve with rice.

SHIME SABA
PICKLED MACKEREL

Shimeru means 'to pickle'; in this case, saba, or mackerel, is cured using sugar, salt and vinegar before being enjoyed sashimi-style or as part of chirashizushi (sashimi scattered over sushi rice). The curing process removes the fishiness from the mackerel, firms up the flesh and imparts a delicate flavour.

Mackerel does not keep well, so it is imperative to check with your fishmonger if it is fresh enough to be eaten raw. It is, however, delicious grilled as-is over charcoal with a little bit of sake and salt, so it can still be used if it is no longer at peak freshness.

SERVES 4 AS PART OF A SHARED MEAL

---

1 × 500 g (1 lb 2 oz) fresh horse mackerel or other mackerel, cleaned and filleted (ask your fishmonger to do this for you), skin on

115 g (½ cup) caster (superfine) sugar

140 g (½ cup) salt

250 ml (1 cup) rice vinegar

grated ginger, to serve

1 spring onion (scallion), finely sliced

grated daikon (Japanese radish), to serve

1   Place the fish, skin-side down, on a non-reactive tray or dish and sprinkle evenly with the sugar. Transfer to the fridge to cure for 40 minutes, then rinse off the sugar, dry the fillet throughly with paper towels and place on a clean non-reactive tray or dish. Sprinkle evenly with the salt and return the fish to the fridge to cure for 1 hour.

2   Rinse off the salt, dry the fillet thoroughly with paper towels, then place on another clean non-reactive tray. Pour the rice vinegar over the fish and transfer to the fridge to cure for a final 20 minutes, turning after 10 minutes to ensure that both sides of the fish are fully cured. The colour of the fish should change from pink to white during this time.

3   Drain the mackerel, dry it with paper towels and transfer it to a serving plate. Using tweezers, remove the pin bones and discard them. Carefully peel off the translucent outer layer of skin (it should come off easily, leaving the inner layer of skin behind) and keep the mackerel covered in the fridge until required, but for no longer than 24 hours.

4   To serve, slice the mackerel thinly, with every second slice going only halfway through the fillet. Serve with the ginger, spring onion and daikon on the side for diners to help themselves.

KATSUO NO TATAKI

SEARED BONITO WITH PONZU

Katsuo no tataki is one of our favourite ways to enjoy bonito, a fish in the same family as mackerel and tuna. The bonito is torched on the outside, then served with a citrusy, salty ponzu dressing. Originally from Kochi, where the bonito is cooked over a straw fire to sear the skin, katsuo no tataki can be found in izakaya across Japan as a starter or small dish.

SERVES 4 AS A STARTER

1 bonito fillet, deboned

neutral oil, for frying

½ onion, very finely sliced and soaked in water for 10 minutes

1 bunch shiso (perilla) leaves

60 ml (¼ cup) Ponzu (page 225)

Braised garlic

1 garlic bulb, finely sliced

60 ml (¼ cup) sake

45 g (1½ oz) caster (superfine) sugar

45 ml (1½ fl oz) soy sauce

30 ml (1 fl oz) mirin

1   First, make the braised garlic. Fill a bowl with cold water. Bring a small saucepan of water to the boil over high heat and blanch the sliced garlic briefly in the boiling water. Drain the garlic, then transfer it to the cold water to refresh. Drain it again and transfer to a clean, dry saucepan.

2   Add the sake, sugar, soy sauce and mirin to the saucepan and bring to a simmer over medium–low heat. Cut out a circle of baking paper the same size as the mouth of the saucepan and place on top of the liquid; this will prevent it from evaporating too quickly. Simmer the garlic for 30 minutes, or until it loses its raw taste but isn't yet falling apart. Remove from the heat and allow to cool. Using a slotted spoon, remove and set aside 1 tablespoon of garlic for this recipe; the remaining braised garlic and cooking liquid can be transferred to an airtight container and stored in the fridge for up to 5 days. This garlic soy can be used as a dipping sauce for sashimi and works particularly well with tuna.

3   If you have a brulee torch, quickly sear the outside of the bonito until charred; otherwise, heat a little oil in a frying pan over very high heat and sear the skin of the bonito this way. Transfer the bonito to a plate and refrigerate until chilled through to make it easier to slice.

4   Cut the bonito into 5 mm (¼ in) slices, with every second cut only going halfway through the fillet to create pockets along the fish. Transfer the bonito to a serving dish, place a slice of braised garlic into each pocket and serve with the onion and shiso arranged on top, accompanied by ponzu on the side for dipping.

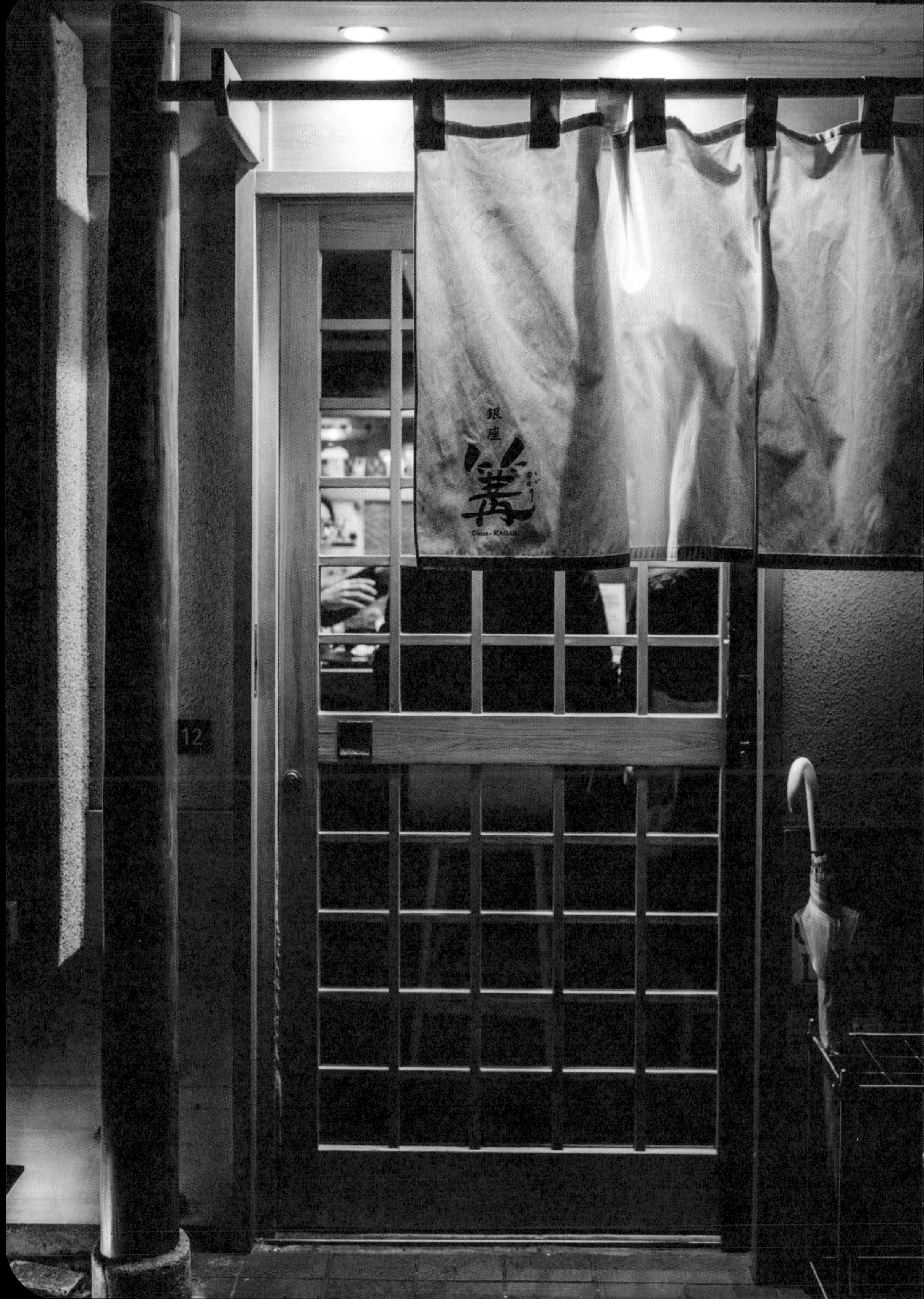
銀座
篝
かがり
Ginza - KAGARI
12

TONKATSU
PANKO-CRUSTED PORK

There is something satisfying about biting into tonkatsu, with its crisp panko breadcrumbs on the outside and juicy, tender meat within. Invented in 1899 by a restaurant in Tokyo called Rengatei (as with most Japanese institutions, this restaurant is still open), tonkatsu remains a firm favourite. Dedicated tonkatsu restaurants purvey the cutlets in teishoku (set meals) and sando (sandwiched between white bread), alongside other popular fried treats such as ebi-furai (crumbed prawns/shrimp) and kaki-furai (crumbed oysters). Most tonkatsu restaurants also have limitless top-ups for the cabbage and rice that traditionally accompany the dish.

Respectable tonkatsu establishments all pride themselves on their secret tonkatsu sauce. We've included a recipe on page 224, but Bull-Dog brand sauce – a Japanese favourite – can be used if you are in a rush. We've also provided a variation to the sauce, a delicious salted spring onion (scallion) mix, which we came across at a very good tonkatsu restaurant in Shibuya.

SERVES 4

4 boneless pork cutlets

2 eggs

1 tablespoon milk

150 g (1 cup) plain
   (all-purpose) flour

60 g (1 cup) panko breacrumbs

neutral oil, for shallow-frying

200 ml (6¾ fl oz) Tonkatsu
   sauce (page 224) and/or
   1 quantity Negi shio (below)

rice, to serve

¼ green cabbage,
   finely shredded

lemon wedges, to serve

**Negi shio (spring onion/
scallion dressing; optional)**

1 bunch spring onions
   (scallions), white part
   only, finely sliced

2 garlic cloves, finely chopped

2 tablespoons sake

1 tablespoon salt

1   To make the negi shio (if using) mix all of the ingredients together in a bowl and set aside.

2   Using a meat mallet, pound the pork cutlets until they are 1.5 cm (½ in) thick.

3   In a large, shallow bowl, whisk the eggs and milk together until homogenous. Place the flour on a large plate, season with salt and pepper and stir to combine. Place the panko on a separate plate and line a third plate with baking paper.

4   Take a pork cutlet and dredge it in the seasoned flour. Brush off any excess and dip the cutlet in the egg mixture, followed by the panko, making sure the cutlet is well coated in breadcrumbs. Transfer to the lined plate and repeat with the remaining cutlets, then place in the fridge until you are ready to fry.

5   Preheat the oven to 70°C (158°F), or as low as it will go, and place a wire rack over a baking tray.

6   In a deep, heavy-based frying pan, heat approximately 1 cm (½ in) oil over medium heat until a few breadcrumbs dropped into the oil bubble straight away, but do not brown too quickly. Carefully lower the crumbed cutlets into the oil. Work in batches to avoid overcrowding the pan.

7   Fry the cutlets on one side until golden brown, then carefully turn and fry again until both sides are golden brown and the pork is cooked through. Transfer the cutlets to the wire rack in the oven to keep warm while cooking the remaining pork.

8   Season the pork cutlets with salt and pepper and serve drizzled with the tonkatsu sauce (if using), accompanied by rice, shredded cabbage, negi shio (if using) and lemon wedges.

BUTA NO SHOGAYAKI

PORK SIMMERED WITH GINGER

Buta no shogayaki is a Japanese household staple: a quick, easy stir-fry of finely sliced pork, sweet mirin and spicy ginger.

SERVES 4

50 g (1¾ oz) ginger, finely sliced

60 ml (¼ cup) soy sauce

60 ml (¼ cup) mirin

30 ml (1 fl oz) sake

2 tablespoons caster (superfine) sugar

1 tablespoon neutral oil, for frying

600 g (1 lb 5 oz) pork, finely sliced

rice, to serve

Pickled ginger (page 25), to serve

green salad, to serve (optional)

1   Combine the ginger, soy sauce, mirin, sake and sugar in a bowl and set aside.

2   Heat the oil in a frying pan over high heat until the oil begins to shimmer. Add the pork, frying on one side until browned. Turn over, then add the ginger mixture and reduce the heat to medium. Simmer the pork until it is cooked through, then remove from the heat.

3   Serve with rice and pickled ginger, and a green salad, if desired.

TONJIRU
PORK BELLY STEW

There is nothing quite as comforting as a bowl of tonjiru on a cold autumn or winter's day. The gobō (burdock root) and root vegetables lend the dish a hearty, earthy flavour, and the fat from the pork belly keeps the broth hot.

SERVES 4

1 × 250 g (9 oz) block konnyaku (konjac gel; see glossary)

1 tablespoon neutral oil, for frying

600 g (1 lb 5 oz) pork belly, cut into 2.5 cm (1 in) cubes

1.2 litres (1 qt 8 fl oz) Katsuo dashi (page 220)

1 onion, sliced

1 daikon (Japanese radish), cut into bite-sized pieces

1 carrot, cut into bite-sized pieces

2 potatoes, peeled and cut into bite-sized pieces

1 gobō stalk (burdock root; see note), peeled if necessary and finely sliced

30 g (1 oz) shiromiso (white miso paste)

40 g (1½ oz) akamiso (red miso paste)

1 teaspoon sesame oil

rice, to serve

2 spring onions (scallions), finely sliced

Shichimi tōgarashi (page 227), to serve

1   Fill a large bowl with iced water. Bring a large saucepan of water to the boil over high heat and blanch the konnyaku in the boiling water for 1 minute. Drain the konnyaku, then transfer it to the iced water to refresh. Drain again and cut or tear into bite-sized pieces.

2   In a saucepan large enough to fit all of the ingredients, heat the oil over high heat. Add the pork belly and cook until browned on all sides, then add the katsuo dashi and onion. Bring to a simmer and cook, regularly skimming away any impurities that rise to the surface, for 15 minutes.

3   Add the konnyaku, daikon, carrot, potato and burdock root. Allow the mixture to return to a simmer, then cook for another 30–45 minutes, or until the pork and vegetables are soft.

4   Place the shiromiso and akamiso in a small bowl. Take the saucepan off the heat, then add a ladle of broth to the miso and mix until the miso is completely dissolved. Pour into the saucepan. (Resist the temptation to add the miso directly to the boiling broth; doing so will overcook it and give the stew a grainy texture.)

5   Stir the sesame oil into the stew. Serve with rice, topped with the spring onion and shichimi togarashi.

Note
If you can't find gobō (burdock root), you can simply omit it from this recipe.

BUTA SHABU-SHABU

PORK SHABU-SHABU

Shabu-shabu is a hotpot dish where paper-thin slices of beef or pork are swished in a hot broth, then dipped into a sesame or ponzu sauce. The dish has its origins in Chinese hotpot cuisine, and was introduced to Japan in 1952 by a restaurant in Osaka called Suehiro Honten. This is a great dish to enjoy with friends, as it is typically cooked in a nabe (hotpot) in the centre of the table.

SERVES 4

1 daikon (Japanese radish), sliced into 2 cm (¾ in) discs

1 × 500 g (1 lb 2 oz) block momen (firm) tofu

500 g (1 lb 2 oz) pork, finely sliced

1 bunch chrysanthemum greens

1 leek, white part only, finely sliced

1 bunch mizuna (Japanese mustard greens)

Shabu-shabu base

2 litres (2 qts) Katsuo or Konbu dashi (pages 220–221)

120 ml (4 fl oz) soy sauce

120 ml (4 fl oz) mirin

Shabu-shabu sauce

110 g (4 oz) shiromiso (white miso paste)

20 g (¾ oz) akamiso (red miso paste)

150 ml (5 fl oz) Konbu dashi (page 221)

1 teaspoon soy sauce

10 g (¼ oz) garlic, grated

5 g (⅛ oz) ginger, grated

100 g (3½ oz) neri goma (Japanese sesame paste; see glossary)

1 tablespoon ground sesame seeds

1 To make the shabu-shabu base, combine all of the ingredients in a large saucepan.

2 To make the shabu-sauce sauce, mix all of the ingredients together until well combined and divide the sauce between four small dipping bowls, one for each person.

3 To serve, place a portable stove in the centre of your table and use it to bring the saucepan of shabu-shabu base to a simmer. First, add the daikon and tofu and cook until the tofu is warmed through. Using a different set of chopsticks from the ones being used to eat, add the pork, a little at a time, swishing it through the broth until cooked through. The remaining ingredients can then be added.

4 Diners can help themselves as soon as each ingredient is cooked, dipping their item of choice in shabu-shabu sauce before eating.

Notes
You can also offer Ponzu (page 225) as a dipping sauce in addition to the shabu-shabu sauce.
   Finely sliced pork or beef can also be found in Asian, Japanese or Korean supermarkets in the freezer section.

GYŪNIKU NO MISOZUKE

MISO-MARINATED BEEF FILLET

Beef is prized in Japan, with various prefectures vying for the best wagyu title. Matsusaka, Kobe and Ōmi are currently the top three, with the pampered cows given massages and fed special blends.

While Japanese wagyu is wonderful on its own, with just a little bit of salt and pepper, konbu (dried kelp) butter or Yuzukoshō (page 226), this take on roast beef with a side of wafu (Japanese-style) wasabi sauce is just as delicious. This dish is thought to have originated in the Edo era (1603–1868), when the consumption of meat was prohibited. The Hikone Domain (now Shiga Prefecture) would marinate the region's prized Ōmi beef in miso, presenting this to the shōgun (military leader of Japan) as medicine.

SERVES 4

50 ml (1¾ fl oz) sake

100 ml (3½ fl oz) mirin

75 ml (2½ fl oz) soy sauce

100 g (3½ oz) shiromiso (white miso paste)

50 g (1¾ oz) akamiso (red miso paste)

1 × 1 kg (2 lb 3 oz) beef rump or scotch fillet

2 tablespoons neutral oil

Wasabi sauce

60 ml (¼ cup) sake

2 tablespoons soy sauce

1 tablespoon rice vinegar

1 garlic clove, grated

1 tablespoon fresh wasabi, grated, or ½ tablespoon powdered wasabi

1 teaspoon sesame oil

freshly ground black pepper, to taste

1   In a small saucepan over medium heat, bring the sake and mirin to the boil. Boil for 2 minutes, then remove from the heat, pour into a container large enough to fit the beef and set aside to cool. Once cool, add the soy sauce, shiromiso and akamiso. Whisk well to combine, then add the beef, ensuring it is well-coated in the marinade. Transfer to the fridge and leave to marinate for 8 hours or overnight, turning once.

2   Preheat the oven to 70°C (158°F).

3   Remove the beef from the marinade, thoroughly pat dry using paper towels and set aside. Heat the oil in a large frying pan over high heat. When the oil is smoking, add the beef and brown quickly on all sides, then remove from the heat and place the beef in a roasting tin.

4   Add 60 ml (¼ cup) of water to the frying pan to deglaze, then pour the juices into the bottom of the roasting tin. Place in the oven and roast the beef for 2 hours, or until it reaches 52°C (126°F), medium–rare, on a meat thermometer inserted into the thickest part of the fillet. If you prefer your meat cooked to medium, take the beef out at 57°C (135°F); or 65°C (149°F) for well done. Cover with foil and allow to rest for 10–20 minutes before carving.

5   While the beef is resting, make the wasabi sauce. Bring the sake to the boil in a small saucepan over medium heat and cook until reduced by half. Add 2 tablespoons of water, along with the soy sauce, and immediately strain the mixture into a bowl. Mix in the remaining ingredients.

6   To serve, transfer the roast beef to a serving dish, accompanied by the wasabi sauce on the side.

GYŪNIKU NO TATAKI

BEEF TATAKI

Tataki means 'to pound', but in beef tataki, the beef is simply seared and finely sliced. It is then lightly marinated in the pan juices and served with a citrusy ponzu sauce and a little wasabi. Usually found in izakaya as one of many small dishes, beef tataki is best enjoyed as a starter.

SERVES 4 AS A STARTER

1 × 250 g (9 oz) beef eye round

1 teaspoon salt

1 teaspoon freshly ground
  black pepper

1 tablespoon neutral oil,
  for frying

60 ml (¼ cup) red wine

60 ml (¼ cup) soy sauce

2 tablespoons mirin

1 tablespoon rice vinegar

1 teaspoon lemon juice

1 daikon (Japanese radish),
  grated

½ bunch spring onions
  (scallions), finely sliced

grated wasabi, to serve

Ponzu (page 225), to serve

1   Season the beef with the salt and pepper.

2   Heat the oil in a cast iron or steel frying pan over high heat. When the pan is very hot, add the beef; be careful, as the oil may spit.

3   Cook the beef on all sides until very well coloured, then remove the pan from the heat, setting it aside for the sauce. Remove any excess oil from the beef with paper towels, then transfer the beef to a plate and refrigerate until chilled through to make it easier to slice.

4   Return the frying pan to the heat and add the wine, using a wooden spoon to scrape up any beef stuck to the base of the pan. Cook the wine until it has been reduced to a sticky glaze, then add the soy sauce, mirin, rice vinegar and lemon juice. Stir until just combined, strain into a bowl and set aside.

5   Thinly slice the beef and dress with the pan juices. Squeeze any excess liquid from the grated daikon and garnish the beef with the daikon and spring onion. Serve with the grated wasabi and ponzu on the side.

GYŪSUJI NIKOMI

BEEF TENDON STEW

Gyūsuji Nikomi is the star dish of the izakaya in the old neighbourhood of Asakusa, just a stone's throw from Sensōji Temple. If you've never had tendon, it can seem a bit confronting, but by the time the stew has simmered for hours, most of the tendon has melted into the rich, hearty broth, leaving delicious pieces of beef behind. In this recipe, we have suggested stewing beef as an alternative to tendon. You can add kimchi to the broth for spiciness.

SERVES 4

600 g (1 lb 5 oz) beef tendon or stewing beef

300 g (10½ oz) konnyaku (konjac gel; see glossary)

250 ml (1 cup) sake

2 litres (2 qts) Katsuo dashi (page 220)

45 g (1½ oz) caster (superfine) sugar

60 g (2 oz) akamiso (red miso paste)

60 g (2 oz) hatchōmiso (see glossary)

1 × 3 cm (1¼ in) piece ginger, peeled and finely sliced

rice, to serve

4 Hot-spring eggs (page 219)

1 bunch spring onions (scallions), finely sliced

1   Fill a large bowl with iced water. Bring a large saucepan of water to the boil over high heat and blanch the tendon in the boiling water for 1 minute. Drain the tendon, then transfer it to the iced water to refresh. Drain again and cut into bite-sized pieces on the larger side, keeping in mind that the tendon will shrink a lot during cooking. Repeat the process with the konnyaku.

2   Place the tendon and konnyaku in a large saucepan and add the sake, along with enough katsuo dashi to cover. Bring to the boil, skimming thoroughly to remove any impurities that rise to the surface, then add the sugar, akamiso, hatchōmiso and ginger. Simmer for 1½–2 hours, skimming regularly to remove excess oil.

3   Serve the gyūsuji nikomi with rice, topped with a hot-spring egg and spring onion.

SUKIYAKI

Sukiyaki was created in Japan in the 19th century, and is said to be derived from gyūnabe, a beef hotpot dish from Yokohama. Once a luxury (as beef was expensive), it is now a popular meal for gatherings, as the dish is typically cooked over a portable stove in the centre of the table and everyone can take part. In Japan, the sukiyaki ingredients are dipped into a beaten raw egg before eating, but here, we use Hot-spring eggs (page 219) instead.

SERVES 4

1 packet shirataki (konjac) noodles (optional; see glossary)

neutral oil or beef fat, for frying

2 leeks, white part only, cut into 4 cm (1½ in) lengths

1 carrot, cut into bite-sized pieces

500 g (1 lb 2 oz) beef fillet, finely sliced (see note)

250 ml (1 cup) Katsuo dashi (page 220)

1 × 500 g (1 lb 2 oz) block momen (firm) tofu, cubed

½ Chinese cabbage (wombok), cut into bite-sized pieces

6–8 fresh whole shiitake mushrooms

rice, to serve

4 Hot-spring eggs (page 219)

Sukiyaki sauce

500 ml (2 cups) sake

75 ml (2½ fl oz) mirin

160 ml (5½ fl oz) soy sauce

1 tablespoon caster (superfine) sugar

1   To make the sukiyaki sauce, place the sake and mirin in a small saucepan over medium heat and cook until reduced by half. Add the soy sauce and sugar and cook until the sugar dissolves. Set aside.

2   Fill a large bowl with iced water. Bring a saucepan of water to the boil over high heat and blanch the shirataki noodles in the boiling water for 30 seconds. Drain the noodles, then transfer them to the iced water to refresh. Drain again and set aside.

3   Heat the oil or melt the beef fat in a large, shallow frying pan over medium heat, then add the leek and carrot and cook until coloured on all sides. Add the sliced beef, cooking until browned.

4   Pour the sukiyaki sauce and katsuo dashi over the beef and vegetables, then arrange the tofu, cabbage and mushrooms on top. Bring to a simmer and cook for 10–15 minutes, regularly skimming away any impurities that rise to the surface.

5   Bring the pan to the dining table to allow everyone to share, serving with a bowl of rice and a hot-spring egg for each person.

Note
To easily slice beef for sukiyaki, place it in the freezer for ½–1 hour, or until just firm but not frozen solid. Using a gentle back-and-forth motion, cut thin slices across the grain for the most tender results.
   Finely sliced beef can also be found in Asian, Japanese or Korean supermarkets in the freezer section.

AMAZAKE
SWEET SAKE

In the chilly Japanese winters, on temple and shrine grounds and especially in the countryside, you will come across stalls flying flags with the characters 甘酒 (amazake) emblazoned on them. The sweet, rice-pudding like drink is incredibly warming in the cold weather and, if you like, a little grated ginger can be stirred in for extra heat.

Despite its name, amazake contains no alcohol. A naturally nutritious rice drink made by fermenting cooked rice with kōji (fermented rice used in the sake-making process), amazake has been enjoyed by the Japanese for over a thousand years. The sweetness is derived from the enzymes in the koji, which break down the complex starches in the rice into natural sugar.

This recipe requires a rice cooker; if you don't have one, they are a worthwhile investment!

MAKES APPROXIMATELY 2 LITRES (2 QTS)

440 g (2 cups) Japanese short-grain rice

300 g (10½ oz) kōji (fermented rice; see glossary)

grated ginger, to taste (optional)

caster (superfine) sugar, to taste (optional)

1 Place the rice and 1 litre (1 qt) of water into the bowl of an electric rice cooker and cook on the congee/porridge setting. If your rice cooker does not have a congee/porridge setting, cook the rice until tender (the mixture will still be quite watery).

2 Once the rice is cooked, break the kōji into small pieces and stir through the rice. Leave the mixture in the rice cooker on 'keep warm' for 6 hours, stirring every 1–2 hours.

3 If not being used immediately, the amazake can be cooled, transferred to an airtight container and stored in the fridge for up to 3 days.

4 To serve, dilute the amazake with water until it has the consistency of thin rice pudding, and heat in a saucepan or the microwave until warm. Add grated ginger and sugar to taste, if desired.

KUZUKIRI TO
TOKOROTEN

Created in Kyoto where the summers are hot and humid, kuzukiri is an elegant dish of ribbons of kuzu (arrowroot) starch dressed with kinako (roasted soybean powder) and kuromitsu (Japanese brown sugar syrup). The chilled translucent strands are wonderfully refreshing in the hot weather, and kuzu – once used as a medicine in Japan – is said to improve blood circulation and digestion, and is rich in antioxidants.

Here, we show you how to make kuzukiri and tokoroten, a close relative. Tokoroten is made with agar-agar (or kanten, as it is known in Japan), a jelly-like substance made from algae. Unlike kuzukiri, tokoroten can be served as a dessert or used as a savoury ingredient; by omitting sugar, it can replace the ramen in Chilled ramen (page 155). Special cutters known as tokoroten tsuki are used to create beautiful, even, crystal-clear noodles, but the kuzu block can also be cut into ribbons with a knife.

SERVES 4

Arrowroot kuzukiri

40 g (1½ oz) kuzu (arrowroot) starch

kuromitsu (Japanese brown sugar syrup), to serve

kinako (roasted soybean powder), to serve

Agar-agar tokoroten

neutral oil, for greasing

100 g (3½ oz) caster (superfine) sugar

10 g (⅜ oz) agar-agar

kuromitsu, to serve

kinako, to serve

1   To make arrowroot kuzukiri, fill a large bowl with iced water and bring a large saucepan of water to a simmer over low heat. Whisk the kuzu with 120 ml (4 fl oz) of water until no lumps remain. Strain into a metal baking tray that will fit into both the saucepan and the bowl; the kuzu mixture should only be 1–2 mm (1/16 in) deep.

2   Taking care not to burn yourself, immerse the base of the tray in the simmering water, making sure it does not come over the top of the tray. Keep the tray in this position until the mixture is set.

3   Once set, fully submerge the entire tray in the hot water for 10 seconds. Immediately transfer to the bowl of iced water and fully submerge the tray in iced water.

4   When cool enough to touch, pull the sheet of kuzu off the tray, place on a chopping board and slice into 1 cm (½ inch) wide ribbons. Serve drizzled with kuromitsu and sprinkled with kinako.

5   To make tokoroten, grease a 21 cm (8¼ in) square baking tin with oil and set aside.

6   In a large saucepan over medium heat, bring 1 litre (1 qt) of water, the sugar and agar-agar to a simmer, stirring constantly until the agar-agar is completely dissolved.

7   Pour into the prepared tin and set aside to cool to room temperature. Once it reaches room temperature, it should be set. Cover with plastic wrap and refrigerate until cold.

8   Once chilled, turn out onto a cutting board and cut into rectangles. If you have a tokoroten tsuki tool, place the rectangles into that and push to cut. Otherwise, use a knife to cut into fine strips. Serve drizzled with kuromitsu and sprinkled with kinako.

CASUTERA
CASTELLA CAKE

This delicious honey cake was brought to Nagasaki by the Portuguese in the 16th century, and traces its origins back to Portugal's pao de Castela, or bread from Castile. Our version is more of a syrup cake, and as such, needs to be made the day before for the honey to soak through. Its light, fragrant sweetness is best enjoyed with a black coffee or tea.

SERVES 6–8

6 eggs

200 g (7 oz) caster (superfine) sugar

20 ml (¾ fl oz) milk

40 g (1½ oz) honey

200 g (7 oz) plain (all-purpose) flour

1   Preheat the oven to 180°C (350°F) and line the bottom and sides of a 23 cm x 11 cm (9 in x 4.5 in) loaf tin with baking paper.

2   Bring a large saucepan of water to a simmer over medium heat. In a bowl large enough to sit on top of the mouth of the saucepan, whisk the eggs and sugar together.

3   Place the bowl on top of the saucepan, ensuring the bottom of the bowl does not touch the water's surface. Continue whisking until the mixture is thick, pale in colour and creamy, approximately 10–15 minutes; this step is easier with a hand-held blender. If the mixture appears to be scrambling before it is thick, pale and creamy, transfer it to the bowl of a stand mixer and whisk until doubled in volume.

4   When the mixture has thickened, remove from the heat and whisk in the milk and half of the honey. Sift in the flour and fold it through with a spatula.

5   Pour the mixture into the loaf tin, level out the top with a spatula and bang the tin on the counter to smooth out the surface. Place in the oven and bake for 40 minutes, or until a skewer inserted into the centre of the cake comes out clean.

6   Transfer the cake to a wire rack and allow it to cool in its tin for 15 minutes. Meanwhile, mix the remaining honey with 2 tablespoons of water to create a syrup. After 15 minutes, turn the cake out, remove the baking paper and brush the top liberally with the honey syrup.

7   Wrap the cake in plastic wrap and leave on a flat surface for 10 minutes to allow the syrup to soak through to the bottom of the cake. After 10 minutes, turn the cake over again to allow the syrup that has pooled at the bottom to be reabsorbed into the cake. Refrigerate overnight.

8   The next day, trim off the sides and ends of the cake to make it look like the ones in Japanese department stores, and cut into slices to serve. The cake will keep for 3 days wrapped in plastic wrap in the fridge.

STRAWBERRY POUND CAKE

This is a variation on the Choc–orange pound cake (page 139) – this time with pistachios and juicy, sweet strawberries.

SERVES 6–8

neutral oil, for greasing

110 g (4 oz) unsalted butter, at room temperature

½ teaspoon vanilla bean paste

130 g (4½ oz) caster (superfine) sugar

2 eggs, separated

20 ml (¾ fl oz) lemon juice

35 g (1¼ oz) almond flour

75 g (½ cup) plain (all-purpose) flour

¾ teaspoon baking powder

35 g (¼ cup) chopped pistachios

100 g (3½ oz) roughly chopped strawberries

20 ml (¾ fl oz) brandy

To decorate

50 g (⅓ cup) pistachios

100 g (3½ oz) icing (confectioners') sugar

25 g (1 oz) unsalted butter, melted

2 tablespoons milk

100 g (3½ oz) strawberries, hulled

freeze-dried strawberries

1   Preheat the oven to 180°C (350°F) and line a greased 18 cm × 8 cm × 6 cm (3 in × 7 in × 2½ in) loaf tin with baking paper.

2   In a stand mixer fitted with the paddle attachment, beat together the butter, vanilla bean paste and 50 g (1¾ oz) of the sugar until pale and creamy. Add the egg yolks and lemon juice and combine. Transfer the mixture to a large mixing bowl and thoroughly clean and dry the bowl of the stand mixer. Affix the whisk attachment.

3   Whisk together the egg whites and 60 g (2 oz) of the sugar until stiff peaks form.

4   Meanwhile, sift the almond flour, plain flour and baking powder into the butter mixture and fold it in with a spatula.

5   Finally, fold the egg whites into the mixture, followed by the chopped pistachios and strawberries, taking care not to overmix. Pour into the pound cake tin, smoothing out the surface but making the sides of the mixture higher than the centre (the cake will rise in the centre).

6   Bake for 40 minutes, or until a skewer inserted into the centre of the cake comes out clean. Transfer to a wire rack and allow to cool in its tin for 15 minutes, then turn out.

7   In a small saucepan, mix together the remaining 20 g (¾ oz) of sugar and the brandy. Cook until the sugar dissolves, then brush the mixture over the cake. Wrap in plastic wrap until cool.

8   To decorate, dry-fry the pistachios in a small frying pan over medium heat until fragrant and slightly coloured, then transfer to a bowl and set aside. In a separate mixing bowl, combine the icing sugar, butter and milk; the mixture should be the consistency of thin cream. (You can add more milk if necessary to achieve the desired consistency.) Drizzle the mixture over the cooled cake, then decorate with the toasted pistachios and fresh and freeze-dried strawberries.

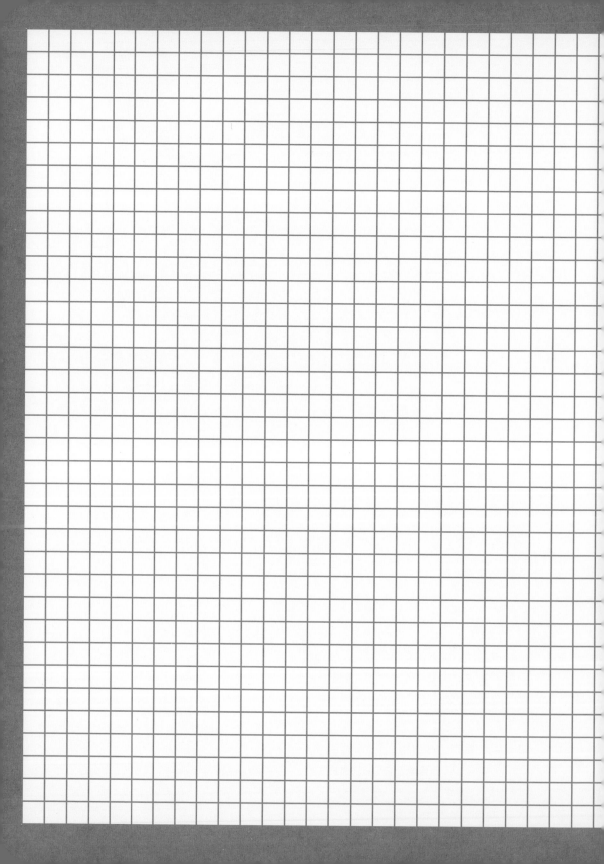

BASICS

SHOKUPAN
MILK BREAD

Our Australian chef friend, who lives in Japan, once made sourdough bread for his Japanese wife and her family. He couldn't easily find the kind he ate back home, and missed the rustic, country-style loaves. He is a good baker, but we can't say for certain that his wife and her family were charmed by his efforts. The Japanese are completely smitten with milk bread, you see, and it's worlds apart from the chewy loaves and hard crusts typical of European breads.

Milk bread is soft, white, sweet and fluffy: the perfect foil for a multitude of fillings, from cream, custard and red bean to katsu (crumbed and fried cutlets; page 186), fried noodles (see page 121) and curry (see page 127). It is also delicious eaten on its own.

MAKES 1 X 2.8 LITRE (95 FL OZ) LIDDED LOAF TIN OR 12 ROLLS

220 g (1½ cups) bread flour, plus extra for dusting

165 ml (5½ fl oz) milk

50 g (1¾ oz) caster (superfine) sugar

10 g (¼ oz) salt

4 g (⅛ oz) dried yeast

60 g (2 oz) butter, at room temperature, diced

neutral oil, for greasing

Preferment

220 g (1½ cups) strong flour

165 ml (5½ fl oz) water

2.5 g (⅛ oz) dried yeast

Egg Wash

1 egg yolk

2 tablespoons milk

1   Start by making the preferment. Mix the ingredients together, then cover and leave for 24 hours at room temperature.

2   The next day, put the preferment in the bowl of a stand mixer. Add all the remaining ingredients, except the butter and oil. Knead on low speed using a dough hook for 5 minutes. Scrape down the side, add the butter and knead for another 10 minutes, or until the dough is very elastic, scraping down the side of the bowl every 2 minutes.

3   To make a loaf, when the dough is ready, scrape down the side of the bowl again, then cover and leave to rest in a warm place for 1 hour, or until doubled in size. (To make rolls, skip to step 12.)

4   Turn the dough out onto a clean work surface and divide into three even pieces. Form each piece into a smooth ball, then cover and leave to rest for 20 minutes.

5   Meanwhile, lightly grease a 2.8 litre (95 fl oz) lidded loaf tin with oil.

6   Lightly flour your work surface. Turn one rested dough ball over onto the work surface so the smooth side faces down. Using your hands or a rolling pin, stretch the dough to roughly the size of an A4 sheet of paper, or about 20 cm x 30 cm (8 in x 12 in). Fold the left side of the dough over two-thirds of the dough. Press down to remove any large air bubbles, then fold the right side all the way over to the left edge.

7   Take the top of the dough with both hands, then tightly roll from top to bottom to create a log. Seal the excess dough by pinching it together, then place, seal-side down, in the loaf tin. Repeat with the remaining two dough balls.

8   Slide the lid on the loaf tin and leave in a warm place for 1 hour, or until the dough has doubled in size.

9   When ready to cook, preheat the oven to 180°C (350°F). Bake the bread for 20 minutes, then turn the oven down to 165°C (330°F) and bake for another 15 minutes.

10 Remove the loaf tin from the oven, carefully remove the lid and turn the loaf out onto a cooling rack. Allow to cool for 30 minutes before slicing.

11 If using the bread for sando, use it within 2 days. It will be fine as toast for up to 5 days.

12 To make rolls instead of a loaf, after step 2, punch the dough down and shape into 12 evenly sized rolls. Place on a baking paper-lined tray, leaving a 10 cm (4 in) space between each roll. Cover the tray with plastic wrap and let rest for 30 minutes to 1 hour or until doubled in size.

13 Meanwhile, preheat the oven to 200°C (400°F).

14 In a small bowl, beat 1 egg yolk with 2 tablespoons of milk to make an egg wash.

15 Pour 250ml (1 cup) of water into a metal baking tin and place on the bottom of the oven. Brush the tops of the rolls with the egg wash and bake for 15 minutes, or until the rolls sound hollow when tapped. Transfer to a wire rack and allow to cool before using. The rolls will keep for up to 5 days.

GOHAN
RICE

Japanese rice is known for being soft, white and fluffy, with a lovely glossy sheen when cooked. The secret is washing the rice beforehand, which removes excess starch, rehydrates the grain and polishes it slightly.

SERVES 2

220 g (1 cup) Japanese
   short-grain rice

1   To wash the rice, place the rice in a sieve and submerge it in a large bowl filled with water. Using your palms, gently rub the rice back and forth in the sieve. When the water turns cloudy, drain the bowl, refill it with fresh water, and repeat the washing process another two times, or until the water runs clear. Drain the rice well.

2   Place the washed rice and 250 ml (1 cup) of water in a saucepan. Let it sit for 15 minutes, then place over high heat. When the water starts to boil, stir the rice once, then cover with an airtight lid and reduce the heat to its lowest setting. Cook for 14 minutes.

3   Remove the rice from the heat and let it rest, covered, for an additional 14 minutes. Gently fluff the rice before serving.

Notes
The ratio of rice to water depends on the rice being used. Generally, when the rice is fresher or of higher quality, the closer the ratio will be to 1:1.

The ratio used here is a general guideline; you may need to add more or less water if the rice is too dry or too wet after cooking.

The resting time is extremely important for rice cooked in saucepans or traditional donabe (claypots). If the rice is not adequately rested, much of it will remain stuck to the bottom of the cooking vessel. Leaving the rice for longer than the prescribed resting time above, especially in a donabe, which holds its heat well, is not an issue.

The quantities above are enough for two people. To serve more, simply multiply the recipe: doubling it will serve four, and so on. The cooking and resting time will remain the same.

TENPURAKO
TEMPURA FLOUR

Tempura flour is a light flour that creates a lovely, crisp batter ('saku–saku!'). It is easy to find in Japanese supermarkets, but can also be made from scratch with the following recipe.

MAKES 400 G (14 OZ)

300 g (2 cups) plain (all-purpose) flour

100 g (3½ oz) potato starch or cornflour (corn starch)

1 teaspoon baking powder

1   Mix all of the ingredients together and store in an airtight container at room temperature indefinitely.

ONSEN TAMAGO
HOT-SPRING EGGS

Onsen tamago were originally cooked in the warm waters of Japan's hot springs – hence their name, which means 'hot-spring eggs'. Simmered in their shells for just over an hour, the eggs develop whites with a soft, silky texture and creamy, runny yolks. They can be enjoyed on their own with a splash of dashi and soy; with rice as a bowl of tamago kake gohan (see page 17); and as an accompaniment to dishes such as Sukiyaki (page 200) and Soy-simmered beef (page 61).

eggs in their shells, as required

1   Heat a large stockpot of water over low heat until it reaches 63°C (145°F) on a kitchen thermometer. Using a ladle or a slotted spoon, carefully lower the eggs into the water. Turn off the heat, cover and leave for 63 minutes, checking the temperature every 10–15 minutes. Using a larger cooking vessel will help keep the temperature stable, but if it drops below 60°C (140°F), you will need to heat the water back up to 63°C (145°F).

2   Fill a large bowl with iced water. Using a slotted spoon, transfer the eggs from the stockpot to the iced water and set aside for 15 minutes. The eggs can be eaten straight after cooking, or refrigerated for later use. They can be kept for up to 4 days in the fridge.

3   To serve, simply crack the eggs into or over your dish of choice.

KATSUO DASHI

Dashi is a Japanese broth made from water, hanakatsuo (dried skipjack tuna flakes), konbu (dried kelp) and shiitake mushroom. A good dashi is the foundation of Japanese cuisine; it is rich in umami and gives dishes extra depth. In kaiseki ryōri, Japan's highest culinary art form, there is always a course featuring seasonal ingredients served in a clear dashi broth, showcasing the technique and skills of the chef in extracting its delicate flavours.

While instant dashi in packet and powdered form can be found in Asian and Japanese grocery stores and is certainly convenient, a good dashi does not take long to make, and is well worth the extra effort.

MAKES 2 LITRES (2 QTS)

2 litres (2 qts) cold
   filtered water

1 × 4 cm (1½ in) piece
   konbu (dried kelp)

1 handful of hanakatsuo
   (dried skipjack tuna flakes)

1 whole dried shiitake
   mushroom, torn (optional)

1   In a large saucepan over low heat, bring the water and konbu to a gentle simmer. Just before the water boils, turn off the heat and allow the konbu to steep for 40 minutes.

2   Remove the konbu and reheat the water to 80°C (176°F), or until very small bubbles begin to form on the base of the saucepan. Add the hanakatsuo and the shiitake mushroom, (if using). Turn off the heat and allow to steep for another 5 minutes (see note).

3   Strain the liquid into another saucepan if using immediately, or into an airtight container for later use. Discard the hanakatsuo and the shiitake mushroom. Katsuo dashi will keep in the fridge for 4 days and is a key ingredient in miso soup (page 29), oyakodon (page 57) and sukiyaki (page 200).

Note
The length of the second steeping time depends on the freshness of the hanakatsuo. After 5 minutes, taste the broth and steep for a little longer if you prefer a stronger flavour. Do not steep the hanakatsuo for more than 10 minutes.

Konbu left over from the dashi-making process can be reserved and used to make delicious salty-sweet Braised konbu (page 25).

KONBU DASHI

While dashi (see opposite) typically includes katsuobushi (dried skipjack tuna flakes), this umami-rich broth needn't be off-limits to vegetarians. In this version, only konbu – a type of kelp – is used. Konbu is sold in large, dried strips and is rich in glutamic acid, the building block of umami flavour.

MAKES 2 LITRES (2 QTS)

2 litres (2 qts) cold filtered water

1 × 8 cm (3¼ in) piece konbu (dried kelp)

1   In a large saucepan over low heat, bring the water and konbu to a gentle simmer. Reduce the heat to the lowest possible setting and cook for 15 minutes, making sure the water does not boil.

2   Remove the saucepan from the heat and set aside for 30 minutes. Strain the liquid into another saucepan if using immediately, or into an airtight container for later use. Reserve the konbu for making braised konbu (page 25), if you wish.

3   Konbu dashi will keep in the fridge for 4 days and can be substituted in any recipe that calls for katsuo dashi (page 220).

BEEF DEMI-GLACE

A popular yōshoku (Western-style) accompaniment, this rich and velvety French sauce can be found poured over dishes such as Omelette rice (page 68) and hamburg steak. The sauce takes approximately 10 hours to create with some supervision, but will keep for up to 1 week in the fridge and 3 months in the freezer.

MAKES 500 ML (2 CUPS)

1 kg (2 lb 3 oz) beef bones

500 g (1 lb 2 oz) minced (ground) beef

neutral oil, for frying

1 carrot, chopped

1 onion, chopped

1 celery stalk, chopped

1 tablespoon tomato paste (concentrated puree)

250 ml (1 cup) red wine

1 bay leaf

3 sprigs thyme

5 black peppercorns

1   Preheat the oven to 200°C (400°F).

2   Place the beef bones in one roasting tin and the beef mince in another. Drizzle the bones and the mince with a little oil to coat and roast until dark brown, approximately 2 hours, stirring every 15 minutes.

3   When the beef is almost ready, heat 1 tablespoon of oil in a large stockpot over medium heat. Fry the carrot, onion and celery until golden brown, then add the tomato paste and cook, stirring constantly, until it darkens. Stir in the red wine and reduce the mixture to a syrup-like consistency.

4   Add the beef bones, beef mince and 1.5 litres (1½ qts) of water. Bring to a simmer over high heat, skimming any impurities from the liquid regularly. Just before it boils, reduce the heat to medium, add the bay leaf, thyme and peppercorns, and cook for 8 hours. Skim off any impurities regularly for the first 2 hours, then sporadically after that.

5   Remove the stockpot from the heat and strain the stock through a fine sieve into another saucepan. Discard the solids. Return the stock to low heat and further reduce the liquid by 80 per cent, until you have a smooth, thick, gravy-like demi-glace that coats the back of a spoon.

6   Serve immediately with your dish of choice, or place in the fridge to cool, uncovered. Once cooled, cover and leave in the fridge, where it will keep for up to 1 week, or transfer to the freezer, where it can be kept for 3 months.

GIN-AN
SAUCE

One of the main sauces in Japanese cuisine, gin-an is traditionally used in savoury dishes such as agedashi tōfu and Savoury egg custard (page 165).

MAKES 550 ML (18½ FL OZ)

500 ml (2 cups) Konbu dashi or Konbu dashi (pages 220–221)

2 tablespoons soy sauce, plus extra to taste

1 tablespoon kuzu (Japanese arrowroot starch) or cornflour (corn starch)

1   In a saucepan over medium heat, bring the dashi to the boil and add the soy sauce. Mix the kuzu with enough cold water to make a thin paste and add this to the dashi mixture. Stir to combine and bring back to the boil.

2   Once the sauce thickens slightly and becomes glossy, remove from the heat. Add more soy sauce to taste, if desired. Use immediately, or transfer to an airtight container and store in the fridge, where it will keep for up to 4 days.

TONKATSU SAUCE

Our take on Japan's popular Bull–dog sauce.

**MAKES APPROXIMATELY
1 LITRE (1 QT)**

2 tablespoons neutral oil,
 for frying

1 onion, roughly chopped

2 celery stalks,
 roughly chopped

1 carrot, roughly chopped

1 garlic clove

100 ml (3½ fl oz) sake

100 ml (3½ fl oz) mirin

300 g (10½ oz) hatchōmiso
 (see glossary)

200 g (7 oz) tomato ketchup

100 ml (3½ fl oz) Katsuo dashi
 (page 220)

1 apple, peeled and grated

1 tablespoon grated ginger

3 tablespoons caster
 (superfine) sugar

½ teaspoon ground cinnamon

½ teaspoon ground nutmeg

1 bay leaf

1 In a large, heavy-based saucepan over medium heat, heat the oil and fry the onion, celery, carrot and garlic until soft but not coloured.

2 Add the sake and mirin and bring to the boil, scraping up any bits stuck to the bottom of the pan. Cook until the liquid has been reduced to a syrupy consistency.

3 Add all of the remaining ingredients and cook, stirring constantly, for 5–10 minutes, until the vegetables are completely tender and the sugar is dissolved.

4 Allow to cool before blending in batches until smooth. The tonkatsu sauce will keep in an airtight container in the fridge for up to 1 week, or in the freezer for up to 3 months.

PONZU

Ponzu is a delicious citrusy and salty dressing used in many dishes. While pre-made ponzu can be purchased from Asian or Japanese supermarkets, it is incredibly easy to make from scratch. Homemade ponzu also tastes different from batch to batch depending on the citrus used, making it just that little bit more interesting than ready-made versions.

MAKES 295 ML (10 FL OZ)

125 ml (½ cup) soy sauce

125 ml (½ cup) citrus juice (such as yuzu, lemon, lime or orange, or a combination), plus the reserved skins of the citrus fruit

1¾ tablespoons mirin

1 tablespoon rice vinegar

1 tablespoon katsuobushi (dried skipjack tuna flakes)

1 × 3 cm (1¼ in) piece konbu (dried kelp)

1   Combine all of the ingredients, including the citrus skins, in an airtight jar with a lid, ensuring that all of the solids are immersed in the liquid. Allow to steep in a cool, dark place overnight, then transfer to the fridge until required.

2   Ponzu is best after 1 week, but can be used after 1 day. If keeping long-term, strain after 3 weeks and discard the solids. The liquid can be kept for up to 3 months in the fridge.

BASIC SALAD DRESSING

A light and delicious washoku (Japanese-style) dressing.

MAKES 100 ML (3½ FL OZ)

2 tablespoons soy sauce

2 tablespoons rice vinegar

1 teaspoon caster (superfine) sugar

1 tablespoon sesame oil

1 tablespoon ground sesame seeds

1   Mix all of the ingredients together until the sugar dissolves and chill in the fridge before using. If making the dressing in advance, omit the ground sesame seeds and add them just before serving.

YUZUKOSHŌ

Yuzu is a wonderfully aromatic citrus fruit with a distinctive tart flavour. It is rare to come by outside of Japan, where households often have a tree heavily laden with the yellow, grapefruit-sized globes in winter. In this recipe, citrus rind is combined with salt and green chillies to create an addictively spicy and tangy condiment, which can be served with fish and steak.

MAKES 275 G (9¾ OZ)

150 g (5½ oz) citrus skin (such as orange, mandarin or yuzu), most of the white pith removed, plus the reserved juice of the citrus fruit

100 g (3½ oz) green chillies, seeded, stems and white membrane removed

25 g (1 oz) salt

1   Roughly chop the citrus skin and chillies. Using a food processor, mortar and pestle, or suribachi (traditional Japanese grinder), thoroughly blend the citrus skin, chillies and salt. Add enough reserved citrus juice to create a coarse paste, and transfer to an airtight jar or container.

2   Yuzukoshō can be stored in the fridge for up to 3 months.

Note
This recipe can be altered to make as much or as little yuzukoshō as you like, so long as a ratio of 6 parts citrus skin, 4 parts green chillies and 1 part salt is maintained.

SHICHIMI TŌGARASHI

SEVEN-FLAVOUR CHILLI PEPPER

Created by spice merchants in 17th-century Edo, shichimi tōgarashi is a blend of seven (shichi) spices. This condiment is typically sprinkled over hot udon, as well as meat dishes like Yakitori (page 158), Soy-simmered beef (page 61) and Oyakodon (page 57).

MAKES 60 G (½ CUP)

2 tablespoons gochugaru (Korean chilli flakes)

1 tablespoon white sesame seeds

1 tablespoon black sesame seeds

1 tablespoon hemp seeds

1 teaspoon poppy seeds

1 teaspoon Sichuan peppercorns

1 tablespoon dried citrus peel (such as yuzu or orange peel)

½ teaspoon ground sanshō (Japanese pepper)

pinch of aonori (powdered seaweed flakes; see glossary)

1   In a frying pan over medium heat, dry-fry the gochugaru, sesame seeds, hemp seeds and poppy seeds until lightly toasted and fragrant. Remove from the heat and set aside.

2   Return the pan to the heat and dry-fry the Sichuan peppercorns until fragrant. Transfer the peppercorns to a spice grinder, mortar and pestle, or suribachi (traditional Japanese grinder), along with the citrus peel, and grind into a powder the texture of ground black pepper.

3   Once the toasted ingredients are cool, mix all of the ingredients together and transfer to an airtight jar or container. Stored in a cool, dry place, shichimi tōgarashi can be kept for a long period of time, until it loses its flavour or fragrance.

GLOSSARY

The following are common ingredients in Japanese cooking that can be found in Asian and Japanese supermarkets or greengrocers.

Aburaage

A thin pocket of deep-fried tofu with a spongy texture, often added to miso soup and udon noodle dishes, and the key ingredient in inari-zushi. Aburaage can be found in the fridge or freezer sections.

Adzuki

Adzuki or azuki are red beans, typically transformed with sugar into a sweet paste and used in a wide range of traditional Japanese sweets. Pre-made adzuki paste (anko) can be found in tins.

Akamiso

Akamiso, or red miso, is a salty miso that is deep reddish-brown in colour. As it is fermented longer than its lighter counterparts, it has a deeper, more complex flavour when cooked.

Anko

See adzuki.

Aonori

Dried, powdered seaweed flakes.

Arare

Puffed rice crisps or crackers made with glutinous rice and soy sauce.

Black fungus

Black fungus, or cloud ear fungus, has a crunchy texture when cooked. It can be found fresh or dehydrated. If dehydrated, the fungus needs to be soaked before use.

Burdock root

Burdock root, or gobō, is a root vegetable with a wonderful earthy flavour. It is high in nutrients and fibre, and is also used in Japan as a medicinal plant. Fresh gobō can be hard to get outside of Japan; it is more readily found in the freezer section.

Daikon

A Japanese radish that comes into season in winter. The bottom half of the daikon is said to be bitter, and the top half sweet. Daikon can be found in Asian supermarkets or greengrocers.

Dried chilli threads

These fine, deep-red threads are actually a traditional Korean garnish called silgochu. They can be bought from Korean supermarkets.

Dried prawns (shrimp)

Dried prawns are tiny (smaller than school prawns) and a vivid orange-red, with a concentrated umami flavour from the sun-drying process. As they are used widely in East Asian and Southeast Asian cuisines, you can purchase dried prawns from brands from these regions if you cannot find Japanese ones.

Gobō

See burdock root.

Hanakatsuo

See katsuobushi.

Hatchōmiso

A dark, almost black fermented miso. It is made entirely from soybeans and has a moderate level of saltiness.

Jako

Dried baby sardines, known as shirasu in their boiled form. If you can't track down jako at your local Asian or Japanese supermarket, you might want to try looking for shirasu instead. (Shirasu can be dry-fried to produce a similar result. If you can't find either, substitute dry-fried whitebait or anchovies.)

Kansui

Kansui, or lye water, is an alkaline solution – usually containing sodium carbonate and potassium carbonate – that is used in noodle-making. It can be difficult to find outside of Asia, but a substitute for kansui can be made by heating baking soda to create sodium carbonate and then mixing the sodium carbonate with water. Some Asian grocers may also stock bottles of kansui, or bags of kansui powder that can be mixed with water.

Katsuobushi

The dried, fermented and smoked flakes of the skipjack tuna or bonito. The smaller, finer shavings are known as hanakatsuo.

Kinako

Roasted soybean flour with a lovely, nutty flavour.

Kizami nori

See nori.

Kōji

Rice that has had the *Aspergillus oryzae* culture added, typically used in the production of sake and amazake (sweet sake). It is easily confused with shio kōji (salted kōji); if making amazake, make sure you confirm with the shop staff that you have the right kōji.

Konbu

A type of kelp that is usually sold in large dried sheets. It is rich in umami and is an excellent source of glutamic acid, fibre and iodine.

Konnyaku

Konnyaku is made from water, seaweed powder and powder from the tuber of the konjac plant. Originally eaten as medicinal food, it is a bit of an acquired taste, with a strong smell and a flavourless, gelatinous texture. It is often used as a substitute for meat in temple cuisine. *See also shirataki noodles.*

Kuromitsu

Kuromitsu means 'black honey', but is in fact a dark sugar syrup made from unrefined kurozato, or Okinawan black sugar.

Kuzu

Kuzu or kudzu is the root starch of the Japanese arrowroot plant, valued for its thickening properties.

Light soy sauce

Japan has two types of soy sauces: a light soy sauce known as usukuchi shōyu and a dark soy sauce known as koikuchi shōyu. The light version has a paler colour and saltier flavour.

Matcha powder

Finely ground Japanese green tea leaves that come in a range of grades, with the ceremonial grade being the most expensive. The culinary grade (cooking matcha) is the most affordable, and perfectly suitable for the recipes in this book.

Mentaiko

The vibrant orange roe of Alaskan pollock, salted and seasoned with chilli. It is slightly spicy, and has a milder equivalent known as tarako, which can be used as a substitute. Mentaiko and tarako can be found in the freezer section.

Momen tofu

A dense, spongy tofu that has been drained and pressed. It is firmer than silken tofu.

Mirin

Like sake, mirin is made from rice wine, but has a lower alcohol content and higher amounts of natural sugar. It is usually a pale golden colour.

Mizuna

Also known as Japanese mustard greens, these have a mild, peppery flavour. Mizuna can be found at Asian markets and greengrocers, and substituted with rocket (arugula) or any leafy green.

Neri goma

A Japanese sesame paste made from roasted unhulled sesame seeds, stronger and nuttier in flavour than tahini.

Nori

A Japanese seaweed sold in large dried sheets. The finely shredded version is known as kizami nori.

Nuka

Nuka, or rice bran, is the outer layer of polished white rice. It is essential for nukazuke (rice bran pickles) and can be found in health food stores.

Panko

A Japanese breadcrumb with a light, flaky texture.

Ponzu

A type of soy sauce with citrus (such as yuzu, kabosu or sudachi) added. It has a refreshing salty and tangy taste.

Saikyo miso

A creamy beige miso from Kyoto that is rich in rice malt. Unlike other miso, it has a naturally sweet flavour.

Sake

Japanese rice wine; one of the fundamental ingredients in Japanese cuisine. There are various grades of sake, including a culinary grade for cooking.

Sanshō

A Japanese pepper also used in the seven-spice blend shichimi.

Shirataki noodles

Shirataki noodles are made from the tuber of the konjac plant, and have a springy, chewy texture. Very low in calories and carbs, they soak up the broth in dishes like sukiyaki, although they do need to be blanched or dry-fried before use to remove their distinctive odour and taste. See also konnyaku.

Shiromiso

Shiromiso, or white miso, is the most common type of miso. It has a mellow, salty-sweet flavour and ranges from a pale to medium beige in colour.

Shiso

Also known as perilla leaf, shiso comes in two varieties: a green variety called aojiso and a purple variety called akajiso. The leaves have a distinct herbaceous flavour, as do the delicate purple flowers, which are typically eaten with sashimi. Shiso can be found fresh at Asian greengrocers or in the refrigerator section of Asian supermarkets.

Shōyu

Japanese soy sauce is known as shōyu. It can be substituted with tamari, which has a stronger flavour and is usually (but not always) wheat-free. See also light soy sauce.

Suribachi

A Japanese mortar and pestle used for grinding ingredients. Suribachi come with a wooden pestle and a ceramic bowl (the mortar), which is glazed on the outside and unglazed and ridged on the inside.

Umi budo

Umi budo, or sea grapes, are a type of seaweed made up of tiny pale-green spheres that contain a wonderful salty burst reminiscent of the sea. Outside Japan, they can occasionally be purchased from fishmongers.

Wakame

Also known as sea mustard, wakame is an edible, leaf-like seaweed that is sold in dried form.

Yuzu

A tart, aromatic citrus fruit that has a flavour somewhere between grapefruit and mandarin. Its juice is sold in bottles in Japanese supermarkets, as is yuzu jam or marmalade, a preserve quite similar to its English cousin.

ABOUT THE AUTHORS

Brendan Liew and Caryn Ng have spent more than a decade travelling to Japan, traversing her cities and rural countryside to explore, learn and live the local culture and cuisine. In 2016, they established a pop-up Japanese restaurant, chotto, in Melbourne, bringing traditional ryokan-style breakfasts to the city. The cafe transported diners to Japan on a cultural and culinary journey spanning old and new, inspired by everything from countryside dinners on the Nakasendo trail, to the food of Japan's far north and deep south, and the animated feasts of Studio Ghibli.

A chef by training, Brendan has worked both internationally and locally – from stints at restaurants including Kadeau in Copenhagen and Benu in San Francisco, to the three-Michelin-starred Nihonryori Ryugin in Tokyo and Hong Kong. He studied the craft of ramen making in Osaka before settling on specialising in kappo and modern kaiseki cuisine.

Locally in Melbourne, Brendan has worked at revered Edomae sushi restaurant Minamishima, Kappo, Supernormal, Golden Fields and Bistro Vue.

INDEX

Published in 2024 by Smith Street Books
Naarm (Melbourne) | Australia
smithstreetbooks.com

ISBN: 978-1-9230-4904-8

Smith Street Books respectfully acknowledges the Wurundjeri People
of the Kulin Nation, who are the Traditional Owners of the land on which
we work, and we pay our respects to their Elders past and present.

Publisher: Paul McNally
Editor: Avery Hayes
Design and layout: Murray Batten
Photographer: Alana Dimou
Stylist: Nat Turnbull
Food preparation: Caryn Ng and Brendan Liew
Indexer: Helena Holmgren
Proofreader: Ariana Klepac

Printed & bound in China by C&C Offset Printing Co., Ltd.

Book 307
10 9 8 7 6 5 4 3 2 1

MIX
Paper | Supporting
responsible forestry
FSC® C008047